D0486549

# THE EPISCOPAL CHURCH
## WELCOMES YOU

# THE EPISCOPAL CHURCH WELCOMES YOU

An Introduction to Its
History, Worship, and Mission

**New Revised Edition**

## WILLIAM AND BETTY GRAY

Introduction by John Maury Allin

The Seabury Press

To
John E. Hines
in thanksgiving for
his courageous leadership

Designed by Paula Wiener

Quotations from the Holy Scriptures are from the New English Bible, © the Delegates of the Oxford University Press and the Syndics of the Cambridge University Press 1961, 1970

Library of Congress Catalog Card Number: 73-17898
ISBN: 0-86683-909-7

FRONTISPIECE: ruins of old church, Jamestown, Virginia *(photograph by William Gray)*

87  88  89  90  9  8  7  6  5  4  3  2 .

# ACKNOWLEDGMENTS

WE are grateful for the help we have received in writing this book. Some of it has come over the years from association with members of the secular religious press like William MacKaye and Betty Medsger of the *Washington Post*, George Cornell of Associated Press, George Dugan of the *New York Times*. Some has come from seminary professors and devoted clergy like the Rev. Massey H. Shepherd, Jr., the Rev. James B. Pritchard, and Rev. and Mrs. Robert Rodenmayer, and the Rev. Lawrence Rouillard. Still more valuable help has come from people in the pews like Jinny and Warren Johnson, Arthur and Mimi Kortheuer, and Bill's mother, Alta, all of whom took time to read some of this manuscript.

Our editor, Robert Gilday, has been most encouraging. We owe the greatest thanks to our friend and mentor, Dr. Samuel M. Garrett, Professor of Church History at the Church Divinity School of the Pacific, who read the manuscript and helped improve it.

Pentecost
1974

WILLIAM AND BETTY GRAY

# CONTENTS

# CONTENTS

# INTRODUCTION

This book is a thoughtful introduction to the Episcopal Church. It offers a service provided a generation ago by the Rev. George P. Atwater. Many who were given or who discovered Dr. Atwater's book, *The Episcopal Church*, were led forthwith into membership, or at least into the process of further inquiry.

Amid the rapid and multiple changes of recent years some familiar landmarks have been moved within the Episcopal Church. A real need has arisen for an updated "lead-in" by a well-informed and experienced guide.

Bill and Betty Gray have dedicated considerable time and talent to providing this contemporary introduction to the Episcopal Church. They open the Episcopal Church from within the community of faith and are well acquainted with the organization and structure of this

Church. They recall and relate the origin and traditions of the Church sufficiently for a proper introduction, allowing for the possibility of future relationships while avoiding any suggestion that one is being introduced to a "has been." Transition and changes are given necessary attention to acquaint a new friend arriving, or a prodigal returning.

Introductions are usually most successful when they prompt inquiry, and when they provide opportunity for additional information. Everyone feels more welcome into any new experience when there is gracious sharing discovered among those who already share the experience.

Loneliness, separation, and isolation being so prevalent and widespread for so many in this world, there is limitless opportunity, even desperate need, for friendly introductions to fulfilling relationships. Many long to enter into a relationship where the uniqueness of each individual can be recognized and appreciated, where love and faith and hope can be shared, and community can be realized.

Observers from within and without the Episcopal Church have noted that at times some Episcopalians, like Jacob at Bethel (Gen. 28:17), seem to be unaware that God is in their places. Inquirers have on occasion faced blank Episcopal stares when they presented the request: "We would see Jesus." (Jn. 12:21)

The Episcopal Church is a complicated household with a more varied membership, a richer tradition, and a stronger faith in Jesus Christ than many members fully appreciate. Often, old acquaintances can benefit from a new introduction, especially when it results in greater self-discovery and an awareness of the life and purpose of this community of Christians.

The way is opened to all. Welcome!

JOHN MAURY ALLIN
Presiding Bishop
The Episcopal Church

# PREFACE

A BOOK devoted to the life and work of a single
denomination may seem in these times to be strangely
contrary to the ecumenical achievements of recent
decades. But the movement toward the "Coming Great
Church" need not be interpreted as a movement toward
uniformity of style and behavior. Whatever centripetal
forces there may be that produce a desire for our coming
together as Churches, they are matched by centrifugal
forces that urge us to retain our local uniqueness, and the
balance these days seems to be shifting toward the latter.
It may be that in our increasingly homogenized world,
which is rapidly assuming the character of one common
technological culture, we relish the particular, the odd,
and the original.

It seems appropriate, therefore, to expose and to

analyze the internal life of a denomination, savoring with appreciation whatever is special to it. As the lives of individual Christians demonstrate, the Spirit works in a diversity of ways, gently resisting too much regularization, and universal truth seems to be apprehended more completely if it is encountered in a variety of embodiments.

Furthermore, an understanding of the history and development of a particular religious body in this country may offer important clues concerning the relationship between religion and society in a secular age. As this nation reaches its bicentennial "coming of age," it faces serious questions concerning its religious and ethical beliefs. These have never received an official expression, but they have been supported by our institutional Churches, and have received the voluntary acceptance of the people as a result of whatever authority these Churches could exert. Such institutions and their authority may now be declining in influence, and as the nation is troubled by deep moral and spiritual uncertainties, and even cynicism, the function of the Churches in our life deserves thoughtful review.

This lucid account of a major denomination, therefore, is far more than a guidebook for visitors to an exotic land. It may serve us all as an introduction to one way by which a group of Christians has tried to adapt an ancient faith to our modern condition. The form of the faith that the Episcopal Church had inherited is one that has had long association with many of the major forces and institutions that have shaped this nation, of which science and democracy are central. As an educated, and what we might call an enlightened Church, with a democratic way of life grafted on its ancient, orthodox beliefs, the Episcopal Church has been something of a laboratory for the working out of religious issues of great significance to contemporary life. Some knowledge of its history, and of the shape of the institution itself, may provide useful insights concerning matters that will continue to engage us all in the foreseeable future.

CANON CLEMENT W. WELSH
Warden, The College of Preachers
Washington Cathedral

# 1

# THE CHURCH IN THE UNITED STATES

THE sign with the words, THE EPISCOPAL CHURCH WELCOMES YOU, reproduced on the cover of this book, has become a familiar sight across the United States. It appears in such diverse places as a crossroad in South Dakota and on Fifth Avenue in the heart of New York City.

The sign tells you that the local Episcopal church is a few miles off the highway or a few blocks up the avenue. If you follow the directions, you will discover that the quality of the welcome you receive depends on the community and the congregation. In South Dakota the sign may point to a very small chapel serving Indians who worship in their native Dakota language and who seat males and females separately. In New York City it may point to a cathedral with an attendance of people who seem to be impersonal, even somewhat cold. But if the visitor perseveres, the welcome in both churches is very likely to be cordial.

The Episcopal Church shares with other Christian Churches the acceptance of Jesus Christ as Lord and Savior. Although it has its own distinctive features of history, liturgy, and structure, these are not equally emphasized in all congregations. It is possible to accept the Episcopal Church for the enjoyment of its way of worship or for the compatibility of the local community, but the quality of long-range commitment will be better satisfied with a knowledge of what makes the Episcopal Church distinctive.

Such knowledge should include the history of the Church in North America, the Church of England as present in the colonies and its influence on the formation of the American Church after the Revolution. It should embrace the liturgy and polity of the Church and the privileges and responsibilities of practicing Christianity as an Episcopalian.

The Protestant Episcopal Church in the United States of America (PECUSA) has grown out of Catholic, Reformed and Protestant traditions. Its Catholic characteristics antedate the Church of England, descending as they do from the "One, Holy, Catholic and Apostolic Church" of the early Christian era, and they exist today in the Episcopal creeds, sacraments, ordained ministry, and ordered service.

The flavor of reform instigated by Martin Luther in Germany, influenced the English Catholic, Henry VIII, and was incorporated into the first Prayer Book of Edward VI. Reform shows itself in limits applied to confession, absolution, and repentence, which were, in

Luther's and Henry's time, areas of corruption and disillusion.

The Protestant characteristics closely resemble the reforms regarding ceremony, sacraments, and Roman influences. These were limited, and emphasis was put on Puritan habits—often requiring the most austere life style—and on evangelism, or the stressing of conversion by preaching. As these influences waxed and waned they left their marks on Episcopal history. The result is a Church offering a Protestant congregationalism within a Catholic structure.

The Episcopal Church in the United States evolved from the Church of England in much the same way that the United States evolved from the British Empire in the New World. The anniversary of the first Anglican Communion in America is celebrated annually at Williamsburg and Jamestown, Virginia. The celebration commemorates the event of June 16, 1607, when Captain John Smith and a group of colonists thankfully participated in the Lord's Supper administered by their chaplain, the Reverend Robert Hunt.

There were two other notable Anglican services which figure in Episcopal Church history. Explorer Sir Francis Drake is believed to have conducted services in 1579 at Drake's Bay near the present site of San Francisco. It is not known whether Drake used the Prayer Book since he probably was a Puritan and rejected the use of printed prayers. It is believed that in 1565 Sir John Hawkins offered prayers in a service on the coast of Florida, and this may prove to be the oldest documented Anglican Prayer Book service in the New World.

There were no ecclesiastical consequences resulting

from these early, isolated prayer services, but with the Jamestown settlement, the Church of England gained a permanent foothold. Public worship was one of the first concerns of these English pioneers; they built a rustic altar and later a church, whose ruined tower still stands.

As the Virginia Colony flourished, the Church of England became the established Church and reflected the motherland's experience with the competing Puritans. Religious tolerance was not countenanced. The Assembly of Burgesses, organized in 1619, provided grants of land to the Church and remuneration to the clergy. Church attendance was compulsory, and blasphemy was a capital offense, punishable by death (though apparently never enforced). Whipping was the punishment for speaking irreverently to the clergy. Contributions were based on the style of dress worn by the members.

In New England, conditions were reversed. There the Puritans were established and the Church of England was unwelcome. The Puritans, often touted for their devotion to religious freedom, were anything but tolerant. They wanted freedom for Puritanism, and they felt free to avenge themselves on the Church of England in the colonies for the severities inflicted on them in England. There were differences among the Puritans, however. The Plymouth Colony was made up of nonseparating congregationalists, and the Massachusetts Bay Colony was made up of Nonconformists. The Plymouth colonists, although they did banish a Church of England priest from their presence, were less harsh, and tolerance made progress among them.

These Puritans eventually merged into congregational churches in which the joining of Church and State was taken for granted. Only Church members could vote, but every citizen was taxed for Church support. The Bible was the rule of faith and law. The culture was harsh, even cruel, and dissent was frequent. Still, a few Anglican churchmen came to New England. History records their hardships. Thomas Morton was expelled because he used a Prayer Book and was of a "gay humor." The Reverend Robert Jordan was imprisoned for baptizing children and using the marriage service. The Brown brothers were sent back to England for using the Prayer Book in their own home.

Such extremes eventually brought reaction from the English government, and after the restoration of Charles II, the Massachusetts Bay Colony received a new charter in 1684 which gave the Church of England the right to exist side by side with Puritanism. Thus assisted, Anglicans built King's Chapel in Boston in 1689. Christ Church, built in 1724, still stands as the legendary church from which the lanterns were hung to signal Paul Revere that the British were coming by sea to attack the colonies.

In New York, the Church had few serious setbacks until the Revolution. When the Duke of York took the settlement from the Dutch in 1663, there was no established Church. There existed a measure of religious freedom that the English retained by charter, guaranteeing freedom of conscience and religion to everyone professing faith in God by Jesus Christ.

In 1696, the English freeholders incorporated Trinity Church and sent their Independent minister, William Vesey, to England for ordination. The Church in New

York thrived until the Revolution when it suffered from its close ties to Britain, but it made the transition with little difficulty when the war was over.

Although Maryland was a Roman Catholic colony, Cecilius Calvert, Lord Baltimore, who held the charter, established religious freedom and extended it to both the Church of England and the Puritans. Under Cromwell an all-Puritan council put limits on Roman Catholics and on the Church of England, but freedom returned with the Restoration. James II, a Roman Catholic, tried to lead England back to Rome, and when the "Glorious Revolution" put William and Mary on the throne, Lord Baltimore, who had opposed them, lost his charter. The Church of England was established in Maryland and there was religious turmoil for the next 75 years until the American Revolution reestablished religious freedom and separation of Church and State.

The colonial Church of England was the responsibility of the Bishop of London, who sent out the Reverend Thomas Bray as a special commissary during the Maryland upset. Bray came bearing collections of books for the colonial clergy. This work led him to establish the Society for the Promotion of Christian Knowledge (SPCK) in 1699 and the Society for the Propagation of the Gospel (SPG) in 1701.

The SPG attempted to provide bishops for the colonial Church. The need was apparent for an episcopal-centered Church: the clergy were without direction, could not be ordained in the colonies, and one in five died during the trip to England for ordination. Lacking bishops, children could not be confirmed. Much as the Church desired bishops, the Puritans and Nonconformists detested them; they had already suffered much from "covetous, tyrannical, and domineering" prelates. Nor was there much enthusiasm for a bishop among Southern Anglicans. It became true that the episcopate could not be transplanted from England to its colony.

On the scarred remains of revolution in the new nation, the Episcopal Church was born. Great numbers of clergy and laity chose to return to England or emigrate to Canada during and after the Revolution. In the South where the Church of England had been established, its property had depended on the British government. In New England it was unwelcome because of Puritan prejudices. In New York, New Jersey, and Pennsylvania, where it was strong, it suffered great loss because of the battles centered there. The stigma of being the Church of the English enemy clung despite the fact that two-thirds of the signers of the Declaration of Independence were churchmen and two-thirds of the signers of the Constitution were churchmen. Above all, there was still no native bishop for this Church built around the historic episcopate.

Although there was no bishop, there were several able and devoted priests. One of them was the Reverend William White, the rector of Christ Church, Philadelphia. In 1782, after the fighting had stopped but before the peace settlement was in effect, White published a pamphlet called *The Case of the Episcopal Churches in the United States Considered.* He set forth many guidelines that were later incorporated in the Church's constitution and he attempted to deal with the need for clergy in the new Church. He proposed that in the absence of a bishop, priests be ordained by priests, at least temporarily. Whether the young Church would have accepted this departure from tradition is an academic matter, for before it was acted upon, another devoted group of clergy developed a plan. In Connecticut, just before peace was proclaimed, in March, 1783, the clergy chose the Reverend Samuel Seabury to be their bishop and instructed him to seek consecration in England.

Foreseeing difficulties, his supporters advised Seabury that if England presented overwhelming obstacles, he should go to Scotland and seek his consecration there from the nonjuring bishops. (These were the successors of the bishops who had refused to swear allegiance to William III when James II was driven from the English throne a hundred years earlier. These political Jacobites were cut off from the English establishment, but not from the perpetuation of the Church.)

In England, Seabury was faced with an act of Parliament that required every bishop at the time of his consecration to take the oath of allegiance to the king, which he could not do. Parliament was not disposed to grant special favors to this visitor from its rebellious colony. So, in the city of Aberdeen on November 14, 1784, after waiting more than a year, Seabury was consecrated by the Bishop of Aberdeen, the Bishop Coadjutor of Aberdeen, and the Bishop of Ross and Moray.

When Bishop Seabury returned he found that clergymen from New York, New Jersey, Pennsylvania, and the South had begun a movement to organize a unified Episcopal Church for the United States. Certain of William White's principles were adopted and written into the Church's constitution. They declared that the Protestant Episcopal Church in the United States was independent of all foreign authority, civil or ecclesiastical, and had full power to regulate its own affairs; that its liturgy should conform, as far as possible, to that of the Church of England, that its clergy should be composed of three orders—deacons, presbyters, and bishops; that canons should be formulated jointly by clergy and laity; and that no powers should be delegated to a general ecclesiastical government except those that could not be conveniently carried out by State Conventions. It was later agreed that all states should have bishops with seats in Convention. Thus prepared, the new Church called its first Convention.

On September 28, 1785, the first General Convention of the Protestant Episcopal Church in the United States met in Philadelphia. It was made up of 16 clergy and 24 laymen elected to represent Virginia, Maryland, South Carolina, Delaware, Pennsylvania, New Jersey, and New York. White was elected president. There were no delegates from New England. Connecticut objected to the failure to require that the president be a bishop, on whose leadership New Englanders set great store.

Though four Northern and two Southern states did not attend, General Convention moved to establish the Church's unity. Committees were appointed to deal with the episcopate, the liturgy, and the constitution. The action bound the Church into one and precluded the formation of many independent Churches in the different states. The next year, favorable contact was established with the Church in England. The necessary act was passed by Parliament, and on February 4, 1787, the

Reverend William White and the Reverend Samuel Provoost, the rector of Trinity Church, New York, were consecrated in Lambeth Chapel by the Archbishop of Canterbury, the Bishop of Bath and Wells, and the Bishop of Peterborough. History records that the new bishops were in New York again by Easter Sunday.

The Church now had the three bishops necessary to maintain the apostolic succession in the United States. It had its own constitution and its own Prayer Book (somewhat modified to please the Church in England). It was now its own master. After two years the New England Churches came into union.

From the beginning certain Anglicans have preferred the Catholic characteristics and others have preferred the Protestant characteristics of the Church. While many Anglicans balanced this heritage, the extreme partisans of the Catholic expression have been referred to as "high churchmen" and the partisans of the Protestant expression have been referred to as "low churchmen." This "churchmanship" contention has plagued Anglicanism through most of its history. The New England clergy were largely high church ex-Tories. The laity played almost no part in the Church affairs, and Bishop Seabury felt that the three bishops should decide all disputes. They were also disturbed because of "doctrinal lapses" in the proposed Prayer Book.

Churchmen in New York, Pennsylvania, and the South were democratic, low churchmen, uneasy with the power of the Connecticut bishop, who excluded the laity from the business of the Church. So even as the Church united, there were factions looking to the consecration of bishops sympathetic to their positions, so that if union failed, they could be independent.

William Gray

A gathering in the churchyard of Trinity Church, Broadway and Wall Street, New York City

The National Cathedral, Washington, D.C.

Messiah Church, Wounded Knee, South Dakota

As these events had been unfolding, the tardily established Church in Maryland was getting underway with the strong leadership of the Reverend Dr. William Smith. While the Revolutionary War was still on, Smith, with clergy and lay support, petitioned the General Assembly of Maryland for the various parishes to continue independently. He needed to provide an ecclesiastical name for the legal application and the "Protestant Episcopal Church" was born legally and, considering the Roman Catholic position in Maryland, reasonably. The word *Protestant* had not yet become the antithesis of *Catholic*, and it is not considered likely that the Maryland Episcopalians intended any denial of their historically Catholic position.

The new Church did suffer one serious loss on its way to consolidation. That was the loss of the Methodists. Methodism was a movement within the Church of England whose advocates put great emphasis on preaching, devotional life, and on the Eucharist as the central service of the Church. The practice was accompanied by an evangelical fervor which many in the Church did not like. When Methodism abandoned the apostolic succession and set its own standards for ordination, separation became inevitable (See Chapter 2). The only other schism, that of the Reformed Episcopal Church, occurred about a hundred years later, apparently the result of a similar conflict. There were other matters pressing, however, as the century wore on.

A wave of irreligion and political partisanship was sweeping the new country and the new Church. Anti-British feeling still hampered the Episcopal Church, and this was aggravated during the War of 1812. Public debates raised such questions as whether Christianity had been beneficial or injurious to mankind and whether there was a God. But once again able priests made a difference.

In 1811, John Henry Hobart was consecrated Bishop of New York, and Alexander V. Griswold became Bishop of the Eastern Diocese, which at that time encompassed nearly all of New England. Two other able men followed: Richard Channing Moore was consecrated Bishop of Virginia in 1814, and Philander Chase became Bishop of Ohio in 1819 and later Bishop of Illinois.

Their accomplishments are impressive, even in summary. Bishop Hobart edited the *Churchman's Magazine*, started the Bible and Common Prayer Book Society, and was a moving force in establishing General Theological Seminary in New York City and the college that bears his name in Geneva, New York. He also began work among the Oneida Indians (See Chapter 7). Griswold was a strong evangelical who strove so ably that by the time he died his diocese was divided into five self-supporting dioceses, and four bishops were covering the field he originally opened.

Moore found Virginia short of clergy and standards of religion at a low ebb. But by the end of his career he had established the Virginia Theological Seminary; his five clergy had grown to nearly a hundred; the Prayer Book was again honored; and personal religion had increased among the people. Chase was a master at opening new fields. After serving the Church in New York, Louisiana, and Connecticut, he went west to Ohio and became bishop. Needing training for his clergy he went to England and collected the money to build Kenyon College and Bexley Hall. After a time he resettled in Illinois and became bishop there.

Growth continued. In 1835 General Convention adopted a resolution that every Christian was a missionary by virtue of his baptismal vows, and that the Church itself was a missionary society. This was the flowering of the Domestic and Foreign Missionary Society, founded in 1820–21 and still the incorporated name of the Episcopal Church. Thus all its members were called into responsibility for its growth.

The new responsibility was accepted. Bishop Jackson Kemper went to Indiana, Missouri, and the Northwest. He eventually became Bishop of Wisconsin and was assisted there by James Lloyd Breck who joined Kemper in the establishment of the seminary known as Nashotah House. Breck then went to Minnesota and founded Seabury Divinity School, now part of Seabury Western Seminary in Chicago; and then he went on to California. Leonidas Polk became the bishop for the Southwest and the Foreign Field of Texas in 1838. He was a founder of the University of the South in Sewanee, Tennessee, in 1860. Expansion and growth were evident everywhere.

Then came the Civil War.

As hostilities spread politically, the Southern dioceses felt it necessary to establish themselves as the Protestant Episcopal Church in the Confederate States. The Church in the North looked on this as a temporary rupture and, at the General Convention in New York City in 1862, the roll call included the Southern dioceses as it always had. It proved to be a unifying action. It was repeated at Philadelphia in 1865. Being thus acclaimed, the unity of the Church was resumed and new work began.

The first bishop to specialize in work among the Indians, Bishop William Hobart Hare, went to the

Dakota territories. Schools were built for blacks, and new missionary work began in Haiti, Mexico, Southern Brazil, Alaska, and, upon annexation in 1898, in Hawaii. American churches like the now famous pro-Cathedral in Paris, were opened in European countries.

There was growth in other areas of Church life as well. In 1871, the Women's Auxiliary (now the Episcopal Church Women) was begun for general missionary purposes (See Chapter 3). The ancient office of deaconess, which had not survived when the Church of England separated from the Church of Rome, was revived, and in 1885 and 1887 the bishops of Alabama and New York ordained deaconesses in the Episcopal Church with the laying on of hands.

The continuing growth brought the number of dioceses to more than 80 in the first 150 years of the Church's life, and cathedral centers began to develop. The first was built in Chicago and was followed by the Cathedral of St. John the Divine in New York City—the largest Gothic building in the world—and the Cathedral of SS. Peter and Paul (the National Cathedral) in Washington, D.C., both still under construction.

Churchmanship struggles continued during the Church's growth, with both positive and negative results. A positive fruit of the Catholic influence was the establishment of monastic orders for men and women during this period. The first American monastic order in the Episcopal Church was the Order of the Holy Cross, West Park, New York. This order was founded in 1881 by the Reverend James O. S. Huntington, son of Frederic D. Huntington, Bishop of Central New York.

The Sisterhood of St. Mary, founded in New York in

1865, was the first American order for women. Its headquarters are now at Peekskill, New York, and Kenosha, Wisconsin. The sisters' primary work has been to conduct schools and hospitals for children. Education, hospital and nursing care, and prayer and religious instruction are the central themes of all the orders in the United States and in some cases in overseas centers.

In 1974 there were 10 such orders for men and 12 for women. The population of the orders has considerably declined in recent years, but some have modernized their habits and are working more closely with the Church at large than was true in the past, when the emphasis was on the cloistered life.

There were also small associations of women deaconesses at work in the Church beginning prior to 1871. However, the Church, because of the doubts of evangelical churchmen, did not deal legislatively with this ministry until 1889 when it passed a canon defining deaconesses and their work. This canon remained in effect until 1970, when General Convention in Houston enacted a new one that recognized these women as the equal of male deacons and extended to them all the responsibilities and benefits of the full office of deacon.

The Church was beginning to develop theological pronouncements toward the end of the century; the famous Chicago-Lambeth Quadrilateral emerged from the General Convention of 1886 and was approved in 1888 by the Lambeth Conference. It was an early proposal concerning Christian reunion and indicated a continuing concern of Episcopalians that the whole Christian Church should be reunited (See Chapter 8).

Such rapid and wide proliferations of interest and

action had brought the Church a collection of boards and commissions that proved difficult to deal with. During World War I, this difficulty became increasingly apparent and, in the General Convention of 1919 in Detroit, a new central administration was formed which employed a presiding bishop and a council.

Before 1804 a presiding bishop was elected, but that year a rule was adopted making the senior bishop in point of service the presiding officer. Now, the proposal was to return to the earlier custom of electing a presiding bishop. The House of Deputies (See Chapter 3) agreed, and a presiding bishop, who would relinquish diocesan responsibilities, was elected for a term of six years. A council was formed to assist him. As organization grew, the Church established an effective Board of Missions and began to deal with housekeeping chores like the Clergy Pension Fund.

During the same period, commissions were at work revising the Hymnal and the Book of Common Prayer. The efforts at revision brought approval of a new Hymnal in 1916, which was further revised in 1940. The third revision of the Prayer Book began in 1913, went on through 15 years of study and legislation, and culminated in the authorized Prayer Book of 1928, the first revision since 1789.

The 1913 convention also established a permanent liturgical commission to receive and appraise proposals for change, and to prepare offices for special occasions. The convention's outlook can be summed up in a remark by noted liturgist Bishop Edward L. Parsons: "Its chief value is that its appointment is recognition of the fact that worship is an ever-growing, ever-changing thing,

Further revision is inevitable." This prediction proved true. The need for a eucharistic liturgy that included psalms and Old Testament readings, and intercessory prayers that mentioned contemporary concerns, became evident. A new trial use service of Holy Communion was authorized in 1969, and despite some highly vocal opposition, this was followed by a decade of trial use of revisions of this and other services. A major revision of the Prayer Book was in process.

Parallel to Prayer Book revision, a new concern of the Church arose for issues drawing from the technocratic revolution, the Civil Rights Movement, and the Vietnam War. Historians may some day want to examine the 1960s as years of unrest which dramatically reshaped the Christian Church. The process through which the Church responds to life in the 70s and 80s had its beginning in the 60s. The question became one of survival and at the same time one of servanthood; a question of whether the Church will try to *save* its life or *give* it for the sake of those to whom it is called to minister.

All this, with the seating of women as deputies and the ordaining of women as deacons, seemed part and parcel of the Church's asserted priority for self-determinism for minority peoples in the United States as well as abroad. The 1967 General Convention, in Seattle, was the turning point.

Presiding Bishop John E. Hines had toured the Bedford-Stuyvesant ghetto of New York City shortly before the convention met. He talked with people in the streets and listened to them. In Seattle he presented a plan which was adopted and named the General Convention Special Program (GCSP). This plan was for the Church to budget about one million dollars a year for programs of minorities in community organization and self-determinism. The Episcopal Churchwomen voted to match those funds with money from the United Thank Offering for the first three years. No strings were to be put on the grants, except that groups had to meet nonviolent standards. Churchmanship and other such controversies of the past were replaced by disagreement on concepts of mission and the appropriateness of funding non-Church-related groups. As a consequence, giving for programs of the national Church was sharply reduced.

For many reasons Church attendance was also declining. Only about 40 percent of people who claimed to be members were regularly going to church on Sundays. Church pews seemed to have more gray heads than long hairs; young people were either captured by secular rationalism, which questioned the basic tenets of the Church, or they were off on a "Jesus kick," which appealed to youth on a highly emotional, evangelical level.

Comparing 1976 figures to those of earlier years, showed clearly the loss in Church membership. In 1964 there had been 7,992 Episcopalian parishes and missions; in 1976 the total was 7,507, a loss of 485 congregations. Baptized members had dropped from 3,647,297 in 1966 to 3,072,760 in 1976, a loss of 574,537. And the total number of communicants at a peak of 2,341,861 in 1968 had shrunk by 1976 to 2,098,785, a loss of 243,076. The bottom had not been reached by 1980, which showed 3,037,420 members and 2,018,870 communicants. The rate of decline, however, was not as great as other main-line denominations, and part of the continuing decline was accounted for by the transfer of some overseas dioceses to other jurisdictions. There were also indications that the Church was taking its mission seriously, changing, revising, restructuring to meet the needs of the day.

Those indications were given form by the General Convention of 1976. In one major action, General Convention changed the language of the canons making it clear that women can be ordained as priests and bishops. Another major action gave primary approval—finalized by a second vote in 1979—to a new Book of Common Prayer featuring contemporary language and liturgy.

Claiming alienation because of these actions, a small group in 1978 dissolved ties to the Episcopal Church and named four bishops to head their Anglican Church in North America. The new church was not given recognition by the Episcopal Church or the Church of England.

Throughout its history, the Episcopal Church has evidenced the inevitability of change in mission and ministry. Along with its strong support of tradition it has also recognized the need for flexibility in keeping God's message and God's people in focus. Its flexibility derives from its parent Church, the Church of England, whose history provides a background for understanding how the Episcopal Church works.

# 2

# THE CHURCH IN ENGLAND

THE Episcopal Church is one of 19 national and independent branches of the Anglican Communion. That is to say, it is an offshoot of the Church of England with its own officials and governing bodies, but it retains the traditional sacramental and apostolic faith inherited from the Church of England. Episcopalians are, therefore, Anglicans.

Anglicans share a common history traceable to the Church in England and its struggles with the Church in Rome in the 15th and 16th centuries, which resulted in the establishment of the Church of England and the beginning of a world-wide communion.

It is difficult to pinpoint the time when Christianity came to the British Isles. Legend has it that St. Joseph of Arimathea journeyed to the islands and may have founded a Christian church at Glastonbury. The Venerable Bede, who flourished and wrote between the seventh and eighth centuries, records in *A History of the English Christian People* that in A.D. 156, Lucius, a British king, sent a letter to Eleutherius, the Bishop of Rome, asking to be made a Christian. Bede recorded: "This pious request was quickly granted, and Britons held the Faith which they received in all its purity and fullness until the time of the Emperor Diocletian."

About A.D. 208 Tertullian wrote of Christians in Britain. In his tract against the Jews, he writes of parts of Britain unpenetrated by the Romans but conquered by Christ. Evidently, the Christians in the island quickly set up diocesan organizations for by 314, Bishops Eborius of York and Adelphius, probably of Caerleon, attended the Council of Arles.

Meanwhile the barbarians were overrunning Europe. Pagan gods replaced the Christian God, and England seemed to be among those nations lost to Christianity. By the time Gregory the Great became pope the Church at Rome had largely abandoned its missionary efforts. As a monk, Gregory had encountered pagan slave boys brought to Rome from Britain and had resolved to send missionaries to their land. On becoming pope in 590 he devoted part of his revenue to buying up these slave boys, so that they might be educated in Christianity and returned home to preach of Christ. But the need was urgent and in 596 Gregory chose Augustine to lead a party of monks to England to convert the country.

Out of fear of what awaited them on the English shore, the monks had asked Pope Gregory to relieve them from the task, but he advised, "My very dear sons, it is better never to undertake any high enterprise than to abandon it when once begun. So with the help of God you must carry out this enterprise which, under God's guidance, you have undertaken; and be assured that the greater the labour, the greater will be the glory of your eternal reward."

When Augustine landed he was met by King Ethelbert and his Christian wife, Bertha, and the monks soon learned that they had nothing to fear from the King of Kent. He granted them a place to live in the town of Canterbury, which was to become the see of the archbishop, the future titular head of the Anglican Communion.

The king was soon baptized, and Augustine went to Arles to be consecrated archbishop of the English nation. In time the Pope sent to him the pallium, a symbol of high office, and he was instructed to consecrate bishops, including a bishop of York who would become an archbishop and would also be given the pallium as a metropolitan. The two provinces of the Church in England are still Canterbury and York.

From the first there was a certain amount of independence exerted by the Church in Britain and allowed by Pope Gregory. After he was consecrated bishop, Augustine wrote a series of questions to Pope Gregory, and Bede felt constrained to record the answers. One had to do with the customs of worship or liturgy.

"Since we hold the same Faith," Augustine wrote, "why do customs vary in different Churches? Why, for instance, does the method of saying Mass differ in the Holy Roman Church and in the Churches of Gaul?"

Gregory replied: "My brother, you are familiar with the usage of the Roman Church, in which you were brought up. But if you have found customs, whether in the Roman, Gallican, or any other Churches that may be more acceptable to God, I wish you would make a careful selection of them, and teach the Church of the English, which is still young in the Faith, whatever you can profitably learn from the various Churches. For things should not be loved for the sake of places, but places for the sake of good things. Therefore select from each of the Churches whatever things are devout, religious and right; and when you have arranged them into a unified rite, let the minds of the English grow accustomed to it."

Christianity grew up with England. The Church in England was established and strong, but it was also independent. King Henry VIII is often described as the founder of the Church of England, but this is a discredit to him and to history. In the first place his was neither the first nor the only expression of independence from the Bishop of Rome. Henry II, in 1164, called the Council of Clarendon to consider a set of constitutions to codify the ancient customs and traditions dealing with relations of Church and State. J. R. H. Moorman's *A History of the Church in England* explains it this way:

> The Constitutions tried to prohibit appeals to Rome without the king's consent, and to prevent clergy leaving the country. They also dealt with the question of criminous clerks, declaring that a clerk once tried, convicted and degraded in a bishop's court should then be punished as a layman and may no longer claim support of the Church.

Thomas Becket, Archbishop of Canterbury, took exception to this play for power by his friend Henry, but he had little support from the bishops. He at first gave his consent to the Constitutions of Clarendon but then repented of his action. The bishops evidently were not upset at the idea of limiting Rome's power, which was also to limit Canterbury's power. Becket had his chance to exercise his repentence, and in October at the Council of Northampton, Moorman says, ". . . he threatened with excommunication any who dared to consent to his trial, and solemnly walked out through the crowd of infuriated courtiers, not one of whom dared to touch him."

Becket went into exile in France but continued to exercise great power. He obtained the excommunication from Rome of the Archbishop of York and the bishops of London and Salisbury, who, in turn, appealed to the king. Four knights overheard their grievances and on December 29, 1170, they went to Canterbury, to which Becket had since returned, and they murdered Becket in his cathedral. Henry II, in an effort to establish his own innocence, condemned the murder and renounced the Constitutions, returning to the status quo. (T. S. Eliot's play *Murder in the Cathedral* concerns these events.)

In 1351 the growing sense of nationalism in England found its expression in the Statute of Provisors, which declared all papal "provisions" to English benefices to be invalid. There was a strong feeling, according to Moorman, that the power of the papacy in England "has increased, is increasing and ought to be diminished." Parliament continued its attempts to lessen that power, and in 1353 passed the First Statute of Praemunire, which attempted to stop appeals to Rome. It provided that the penalties of outlawry would be applied to anyone who took to a foreign court any matter which could be settled in the king's court. This was strengthened in 1365 with an act extending the penalties of the First Statute to anyone who attempted to obtain benefices or citations from Rome, and the ancient practice of paying "Peter's Pence" was suspended for a time. Parliament passed a Second Statute of Provisors and a Second Statute of Praemunire in 1393, giving more teeth to the first.

The Church-State struggle was a political reality by 1509 when a 17-year-old boy became Henry VIII, King of England, now a strong and unified country. He was gifted, a theologian of some ability, and a friend of the Church. He became closely allied with Cardinal Wolsey, Archbishop of York. Henry made him the ultimate authority of the Church in England, eclipsing the traditional power of the Archbishop of Canterbury.

About the same time, in 1517, Martin Luther was active on the continent and before long his teachings challenging the authority of the Church in Rome had reached the shores of England. Theologians of Cambridge, including the future Archbishop of Canterbury, Thomas Cranmer, discussed his doctrine of justification by faith and seemed to be generally enthusiastic about this new wind from Germany. But Henry was not pleased. He attacked Luther's position on the sacraments, earning the pleasure of the Pope who named him "Defender of the Faith," one of the extant titles of the English monarchy.

Henry's troubles with Rome, which resulted in his excommunication, are not simple of explanation and cannot be separated from the political reality of the day. The king needed a son as heir. His first wife, Catherine, reached 40 in 1527, having borne him three sons, who had died in infancy, and two daughters. Only one, Mary, was alive. Henry had married Catherine only after a special dispensation from Pope Julius II, as she was the widow of his deceased brother, Arthur.

The pressure was high for a male heir, and Anne Boleyn was present as a lady of the court. Henry entered into a relationship with her and tried to get the Pope to annul his marriage to Catherine because of his having transgressed the laws of God when he entered into the union in the first place. The inhibition of Pope Clement VII to act was as much political as theological, as he was virtually a prisoner of Emperor Charles V, a nephew of Catherine. Henry asked Wolsey to help, but Wolsey was a cardinal and loyal to the Pope. When Wolsey failed to act, Henry had him indicted in 1530 under the Statute of Praemunire for having taken orders from a foreign power. Wolsey the all-powerful had taught Henry a lesson in power, and Henry was to prove himself stronger than the cardinal and the Pope in getting his way.

By 1531, after waiting four years for the dissolution of his marriage, Henry got into a tiff with the clergy which resulted in his obtaining more power. He accused them all under the Statute of Praemunire, for having accepted Wolsey as legate. Then he allowed them to save themselves from punishment on payment of 100,000 pounds and acknowledgment of him as "Protector and Supreme Head of the English Church and clergy." They would not go that far, but in the end they acknowledged him as "Singular Protector, and Supreme Lord, as far as the law of Christ allows, even Supreme Head of the Church in England." Henry then took a parliamentary route. Playing to a growing anticlericalism in the nation, he put through seven bills between 1532 and 1534 which finally separated England from the Church in Rome. In the meantime, he had the Pope agree to the appointment of Thomas Cranmer as Archbishop of Canterbury in 1532. In 1533 Henry was secretly married to Anne Boleyn, who was pregnant. He had to get rid of his first wife. The Acts of Restraint of Appeals set the final stage. This ended all appeal of ecclesiastical cases to Rome and asserted "this realm of England is an empire," thus proclaiming it to be an independent, sovereign state, free of the Holy Roman Empire. Cranmer then, with no appeal to Rome, could nullify Henry's marriage to Catherine. He did so on May 23, and on July 11 Pope Clement VII responded with a decree of excommunication for Henry.

The Archbishop of Canterbury, on passage of the Dispensations Act, was empowered to grant dispensations and licenses, which was formerly a papal power. The act also abolished the payment of "Peter's Pence" which meant that money ceased to flow from England to Rome.

The king's supremacy over the Church was the subject of the Supreme Head Act. The clause ". . . as far as the law of Christ is concerned" was dropped from his title, and he was also empowered to define doctrine and to punish heresy.

The man in the pew was virtually untouched by the king's maneuvers. He had to swear allegiance to the king, but his Church life did not seem much different. The mass was in Latin in most instances, and even though there was a Reformation Party, highly influenced by conditions on the Continent, it did not make much headway with Henry, who was a strong Catholic in tradition and theology.

Henry moved against the monasteries for economic gain; he enabled the publication of a Bible in English, now known as the Great Bible; but he also, in 1539, issued the Six Articles Act that set the doctrine to be believed by the people and that made doubt or heresy a felony. The six subjects were the truth of the doctrine of transubstantiation; the adequacy of Communion in one kind; the necessity of clerical celibacy; the obligation of ex-nuns and lay brothers to observe vows of chastity; the importance of private masses; and the necessity of sacramental confession. This reinforcement of Catholic doctrine, coupled with the Reformation on the Continent and the growing Protestantism in England, combined to create much uncertainty in the land, provided some victims for the stake, and set the stage for some bloody years before Elizabeth I completed the reformation now known as the Elizabethan Settlement.

William P. Haugaard, an author who has explored the Elizabethan contribution, wrote in *Elizabeth and the English Reformation*: "The Elizabethan settlement did not arise out of a vacuum. The English Church passed through the most turbulent period of its life in the thirty years before Elizabeth began to rule. Her reign brought a stability solidly based upon a unique combination of elements drawn from that Church's recent and most distant past."

When Henry died, his sickly son Edward VI ascended to the throne. The nine-year-old had been educated as a Protestant and was identified with the reforming party. Now the man in the pew could tell the difference. The first Prayer Book of 1549 replaced Latin with English; Holy Communion was ordered by Parliament to be administered in both kinds (bread and wine); images were ordered destroyed to end the possibility of idolatry; and Bible readings in English were expanded in worship.

Edward did not live long, and in 1553, Mary, daughter of Henry's first wife and a fanatical Roman Catholic, became Queen of England. She immediately put aside Edward's reforms. She dropped the title of Supreme Head, but acted supremely to restore the old order: Latin, images, altars, vestments, no English prayer books. In 1554 Mary brought England back into the papal realm.

Mary married Prince Philip of Spain and welcomed Cardinal Pole, an Englishman who had been on the Continent since he broke with Henry, and he, in the name of the Pope, absolved the realm from its schism. Parliament had passed the Act of Repeal, which annulled all ecclesiastical legislation since 1528 except the dissolution of the monasteries. The Pope had agreed to let the Englishmen keep the monastic property, ill-gotten by Henry when he needed money.

History remembers her reign as that of "Bloody Mary" because the persecutions of persons who had been allied with the reforming party were fierce. One of the first to die was the Archbishop of Canterbury, Thomas Cranmer, author of the Prayer Book, who was burned at the stake. His see was occupied by Reginald Pole, who, although a cardinal, had not been ordained a priest until the day previous to his consecration as archbishop.

Mary died in 1558, and 12 hours after her death, Archbishop Pole, who had been in ill health, also died. He had by that time fallen from favor with Rome, whose new Pope, Paul IV, was an old enemy. The way was clear for Elizabeth not only to become queen, but also to appoint her ecclesiastical right arm, Matthew Parker, Archbishop of Canterbury.

The Elizabethan Settlement draws its name from two acts passed by Parliament in 1559: the Act of Supremacy and the Act of Uniformity. The first act restored the chalice to the laity; required an oath of all clergy and lay officials acknowledging Elizabeth as "supreme governor" of Church and State; and again abolished jurisdiction in England of any foreign person. The second act reintroduced the Prayer Book of 1552 from Edward's reign, but coupled it with the earlier and first Prayer Book of 1549, allowing for the use of eucharistic vestments and omitting the "Black Rubric" which explained that the requirement of kneeling for Communion did not suggest that "any adoration is done or ought to be done, either unto the sacramental bread and wine there bodily received, or to any real and essential presence there being of Christ's natural flesh and blood."

In 1570, Pope Pius V, failing in his efforts to help Mary of Scotland replace Elizabeth, excommunicated Elizabeth and dispensed all her subjects from their oath of allegiance to her. He issued a bull, *Regnans in excelsis*, and destroyed any hope of reconciliation by placing Catholics in the odious position of having to choose between the Pope in Rome or the Queen of England. If they chose the Queen, they would be excommunicated. If they chose the Pope, they faced death as traitors. Parliament replied by making it high treason to publish the bull in England and by prohibiting holy pictures, crosses, beads, and other "superstitious things from a Bishop of the See of Rome from being imported into England."

The Church of England, born as much out of political and economic disagreement as out of theological differences, was now a fact. It continued its own assessment of itself as part of the Holy Catholic Church as it does to this day, maintaining the apostolic succession, the sacramental priesthood, and many other traditional practices and doctrines, but never again giving allegiance to the Bishop of Rome as Supreme Head of the Church. As the British Empire expanded around the world, the Church of England followed the flag, setting up chaplaincies in foreign lands. Three great missionary societies were responsible for turning those early chaplaincies into full-blown missionary efforts. The Society for the Propagation of the Gospel in Foreign Parts (SPG), the Church Missionary Society (CMS), and the Universities Mission to Central Africa (UMCA) have been the real leaders in building the Church abroad, including the New World colonies.

While the Protestant Churches were being rent by schism after schism, with new sects starting from break-off groups—the Protestant congregational polity allowed for congregations to exert independence with little difficulty—the Church of England held its unity except for one major separation. That one resulted in one of the largest Protestant Churches of this day, the Methodist.

In 1726, John Wesley, a young Anglican priest who was a tutor at Lincoln College, Oxford, joined a group of friends who called themselves Methodists. Their method was to follow strictly the rubrics of the Prayer Book, including weekly Communions, saying the daily offices of Morning and Evening Prayer, and adopting a personal discipline of prayer and fellowship.

The Methodists insisted on their members remaining loyal to the Church of England, and so they set the times for their meetings at hours that did not interfere with the regular worship hours of the established Church. John Wesley tried his vocation as a missionary in Georgia in 1735, but he was not successful and in 1738 returned to England. On May 24 of that year he experienced his "conversion" while listening to a sermon on justification by faith.

His conversion moved him to travel the British Isles preaching to great evangelistic gatherings, as well as to small groups. He wrote a journal of these travels, a truly exciting book, and from his entries it has been estimated that in 52 years he covered 225,000 miles and preached 40,000 sermons. His success in England earned him the hostility of his fellow clergy who were neither ready nor able to take in his form of evangelism. He was often physically attacked, and he found that Anglican pulpits were denied him in many places.

A counterforce to strict, evangelical observance in the Church was the Oxford Movement, which had its beginnings in a sermon by John Keble, "National Apostasy," which attacked a bill introduced in Parliament to reduce the number of bishops in Ireland from 22 to 12, thereby saving a considerable amount of taxation. The bill was reasonable, considering the small number of Anglicans in Ireland and the large number of Roman Catholics who were being required to support the Church of England there. Keble objected that the bill had come from the secular faction and saw that as a threat to the Church.

Out of Oxford came the *Tracts for the Times*, which called the Church back to its Catholic traditions. The Oxford Movement came at a time of ferment and the tracts gained considerable attention. One of the authors, John Henry Newman, raised the argument that the Church of England was a branch of the Catholic Church and was pursuing a *via media*—the title of one of his tracts—between Rome and Protestantism. Newman's *Tract 90* attempted to rationalize the first 14 of the Thirty-nine Articles as condemning Roman *practices* rather than the official *doctrine* of Catholicism. This was hard to accept, and the movement came under heavy attack, especially since many saw it as a movement toward a return to Rome.

Unlike the Methodist schism, a whole body of people did not leave the Church of England, but certain individuals did. Newman was no longer able to stay in the Church, and in 1845 he was received into the Church of Rome. He later became a cardinal and the author of *Apologia pro Vita Sua*, an important theological work of his day. Newman served the Roman Catholic Church in England, but he never seemed absolutely comfortable and he became as critical of the Vatican as he had been of Canterbury.

There were also ideological and social forces that

attracted strong adherents to the Church. One name that stands out is that of William Wilberforce, who was a prime mover against slavery. Wilberforce, a layman, was a member of the Clapham Evangelicals who mounted a sharp attack against slavery. This was, in turn, supported by the vested economic interests of the day—people also connected with the Church of England. In 1807, twenty years after Wilberforce began the battle, the antislavery campaign was victorious. Parliament voted 283 to 16 to declare slave trade illegal and in 1833 to abolish slavery throughout the British dominions.

Another person whose name deserves attention is J. Frederick Dennison Maurice, who offered workmen Christian socialism as an alternative to Marxism. At about the same time that Karl Marx was writing *Das Kapital* (1867) Maurice, who had written *The Kingdom of Christ or Letters to a Quaker concerning the Principles, Conceptions and Ordinances of the Catholic Church*, was Knightsbridge Professor of Moral Philosophy at Cambridge and vicar of St. Edward's there. His theological position was that Christ came to establish the Kingdom, not a sect or a Church. The Kingdom was for all men, with no class distinctions, no rich or poor, and the law of Christ would govern the lives of men. Thus was born Christian socialism, which has had many adherents ever since.

There have continued to be notable Church leaders to the present. One of the great archbishops, William Temple, served Canterbury only two years (1942 to 1944), but during his ministry he became known as a person who understood the meaning of the Church in the world. Temple influenced the political and social life of

England. At least one writer believed him to be the most intellectually brilliant archbishop since Anselm. His deep understanding of liturgy and the universe can be discovered in *Nature, Man and God*, one of his many books. Temple served as Archbishop of Canterbury during World War II, and never, in his BBC broadcasts, would he pray for England's victory, as he could not believe that God could favor either side when Christians were fighting Christians.

The influence of the Church of England has been felt around the world. Chaplaincies developed into full-blown national Churches, none of which were large in numbers of members in comparison with other Christian bodies, but nevertheless they appealed to persons of stature who did have power. The Nippon Sei Ko Kai (Holy Catholic Church of Japan), for instance, has influenced the government welfare programs in Japan, but its numbers are very small indeed, less than one-half of 1 percent of the people.

Today's globe-trotter is likely to find an Anglican church in every large city in many of the countries of the world. The congregation will be indigenous, using the Prayer Book in the common language of the country. The visitor should feel at home at these services. Obviously in areas where there are still English-speaking populations, the Anglican Church is more than likely to have English services.

It is out of this tumultuous but productive experience that the Protestant Episcopal Church in the United States of America, also known as the Episcopal Church, was born.

# 3

# STRUCTURE

THE structure of the Episcopal Church dates back to the early Christian dioceses around the Mediterranean Sea. Paul's letters to the Ephesians, Corinthians, and Galatians were written to people who lived in such congregations. Later there were churches in Rome and Athens and Alexandria and other centers of commerce.

The earliest congregational structure was based on the Jewish synagogue that grew out of the exile of the Jews from Jerusalem some 200 years before the birth of Christ. Ten men could get together and form a synagogue, employing a rabbi or chief teacher for instruction. A number of synagogues in a town could form a representative body with an elected president who would meet regularly with a council to formulate policies related to the synagogues involved.

The Catholic Church structure of dioceses and parishes grew out of this ancient order, and the Episcopal

Church follows that structure. A bishop presides over a geographical entity known as a diocese, and a council meets regularly with the bishop to direct the diocese. Each bishop is consecrated by at least three other bishops and the lineage can be traced to the apostles in an unbroken succession.

The diocese is the most important unit of the Episcopal Church. It is based on geography, generally, but also on Church population, so that dioceses may have borders contingent with state boundaries, or there may be a number of dioceses in a state because of population growth. Dioceses are made up of parishes, which are self-supporting congregations, and missions, which receive financial aid. It is in these local congregations that most Episcopalians have their Church involvement.

It is likely, therefore, that most Episcopalians will know more about their local communities than about the larger structures. Many will have no involvement beyond the local boundaries. However, since they are Episcopalians they bear a share of the responsibility for the support of the diocesan and national structures. This means that to be an Episcopalian is to be something more than a member of a local group of Christians, and it demands a greater awareness of larger responsibilities.

The structure of the Episcopal Church is based on canon law that has come down over the years and has been frequently revised to meet new requirements. Local congregations are under regulations written and revised by larger bodies of lay and clerical representatives, which means that an Episcopal Church congregation cannot exist and operate independently of the whole; it exists because of the whole.

This is a structure that derives from a rural concept

intended to facilitate communication between bishop and people, but it has become a problem as the world has changed from rural to urban patterns. Congregations are no longer isolated groups of parishoners coming down country lanes from scattered farms to worship together on Sundays. There is clearly a need for restructure to meet the urban situation.

Parishes operate with a rector or priest-in-charge. He is the chief administrative officer and works in concert with a vestry made up of elected representatives of the congregation. Larger parishes may have a multiplicity of clergy and laity on their staffs. However, most parishes are small, with membership of 100 or less. They have one priest and sometimes a part-time secretary, and they depend on volunteers to do most of the work. Assisting clergy are called assistants or curates, and they may be deacons as well as priests.

The size of the vestry is determined by the parish or by Canon Law and is usually a group of nine to fifteen men and women. They are charged with the temporal affairs of the congregation and they meet monthly, with the rector presiding. Officers of the vestry are two wardens, senior and junior, and the clerk or secretary. The treasurer may or may not be a member of the vestry, depending on local custom. Often the junior warden is responsible for the church property.

Parishes are expected to give a certain amount of their income for work outside their boundaries, usually through the diocese. This includes support of the episcopate. Some dioceses have assessments and quotas for each parish, based on mathematical formulae; others are on a volunteer system with vestries determining how much of the parish income will be passed along to the wider work. This is often based on some percentage commitment and some parishes try to give to others as much as they spend on themselves.

Since the budget is so important, vestries spend considerable time on income and expenses and on writing the annual budget. They set the salary scales and are responsible for raising the money to meet expenses. Even though they are charged heavily with the temporal responsibility, most vestries are also brought into the whole operation of the local parish, heading up liturgical committees and other program groups. Some parishes have councils relating to programs, and members of the vestry serve on these and provide liaison with the larger body.

Vestries also have the important job of finding a new rector whenever a vacancy occurs. This process is not an exact science, and since there usually is an abundance of clergy, vestries have an opportunity to find the person who really meets their needs. Bishops and diocesan ministries commissions help in the location of a new clergyman and the Church Deployment Office at the National Church headquarters is also a helpful resource. There are consultation organizations, too, that will consult with vestries on a fee basis to help match the right man with the job.

It is difficult for a parish to sever its relationship with a rector. The vestry can ask the rector to resign, and if he refuses, the bishop can be invited to step in and sever the relationship. A clergyman may resign at any time, but otherwise he is called for an indefinite curacy. A congregation enables a clergyman to exercise ministry; it does not employ him in the legal sense. This is acknowledged by the Internal Revenue Service, which recognizes clergy as self-employed people.

Another type of local congregation is the mission. This is not a self-supporting group but receives a subsidy through the diocesan treasurer. Even so, it has an assessment to meet because Episcopalians are expected to give outside their local boundaries for the wider mission of Christ's Church. Missions are in the charge of a priest or deacon who is called the vicar. He is appointed by the bishop, is directly under his control, and can be moved by him.

Most new congregations start as missions, and many dioceses require them to remain so for at least two years even though they may have enough income to be self-supporting. In this way the diocese is able to have a say in the location of missions and to provide the backing necessary to assure the new congregation of getting a strong start. Some missions never become parishes because they are located in communities without growth potential or that are economically unable to become self-supporting. There is no taint to this situation since the nature of the diocesan system is one of sharing, and the mission of the Church is to be served wherever it is, without the pressure of each and every congregation having to support itself.

There are also parishes that cannot pay all their expenses and therefore require a subsidy, usually temporarily, from the diocese. When a parish gets into financial difficulty, it can revert to mission status, but is usually reluctant to do that if it can carry on for a time with diocesan aid. The parish may have to turn its property ownership as well as other authority over to the diocese, and most congregations would rather continue enjoying whatever independence they can.

Parishes are directly related to the diocese through representation at the annual diocesan convention. Some convention delegates are named by the vestry; some are elected by the congregation at the annual parish meeting. All canonically resident clergy have a vote in the diocesan convention. The number of lay delegates is usually dependent on the size of the congregation and the particular requirements of the diocese. The diocesan convention, over which the bishop presides, sets the program budget for the diocese for the fiscal year. It also elects bishops whenever vacancies exist, persons to diocesan committees and councils as required, and deputies to the General Convention of the Church.

Dioceses have interim committees, or councils, which meet regularly with the bishop to carry out the policies of the convention and to do whatever else is necessary to operate the diocese between meetings of the convention. This is an ancient tradition, recognizing that a bishop's authority is grounded in his council, and is not unilateral.

The most important committee of a diocese, canonically, is the Standing Committee, which runs the diocese if a vacancy occurs in the episcopate by the death or resignation of the bishop. It also approves applications of persons for candidacy to study for holy orders, and for ordination to the diaconate and priesthood. The Standing Committee is called to give its consent to the election of bishops by other dioceses; majority approval is required before an election can be held and the results ratified.

The fact that every bishop and Standing Committee has to vote on approval of the election of another bishop in another diocese indicates how interrelated and interdependent the dioceses are. The bishops sit in the House of Bishops which meets annually. A diocese not only elects its bishop as its head, but also, on that election, places the bishop in the House. The election process allows members of the House to say "yes" or "no" to a new member. This has given the House of Bishops the aura of an exclusive club, and sometimes it seems to act that way. On the other hand, however, the relationship of the bishops to each other is what makes the Episcopal Church, indeed the Anglican Communion, what it is. This arrangement means that all diocesan bishops are equal in authority even though they may have decided to relinquish some of their authority to a larger body in favor of a greater unity in the Episcopal Church.

Here is where the importance of Communion, not only as a sacrament of strength and renewal but as the focus of ecclesiastical discipline, comes into play. Episcopalians are people who are in communion with a diocesan bishop. The Episcopal Church is a body of bishops who are in communion with each other and with members of the various dioceses. The Anglican Communion is a group of national Churches whose bishops are in communion with the Archbishop of Canterbury. Thus an Episcopalian is in communion with the Archbishop of Canterbury and, therefore, in communion with every other Anglican. This means that an Episcopalian is welcome to communicate, to receive the Body and Blood of Our Lord, at the altar of any Anglican church, as well as at the altars of some churches of the wider Episcopal fellowship: The Old Catholic Churches of Europe, Church of South India, Lusitanian Catholic Church in Portugal, Mar Thoma Syrian Church of Malabar (India), United Church of North India, United Church of Pakistan, Philippine Independent Church, Spanish Reformed Church, Church of Finland, and Church of Sweden.

Some dioceses have more than one bishop. Some, such as Montana, are huge in territory, and others are huge in membership and congregations. One bishop cannot fulfill all his obligations and will require assistants. There are two types of assistant bishops elected in the Episcopal Church: the coadjutor and the suffragan. Both have been given full voice and vote in the House of Bishops and full ecclesiastical authority. They can confirm and ordain and participate in the consecration of new bishops. The duties of coadjutor and suffragan bishops are set by the diocesan.

The coadjutor bishop is elected by the diocesan convention on request of the diocesan bishop, usually a few years before the latter's retirement. The coadjutor automatically succeeds the diocesan at the time of his retirement, or if some other contingency vacates the office. At the time of his election, the coadjutor is given certain authority—spelled out in the election call—and this authority cannot be recalled by the diocesan.

Suffragan bishops are truly assistants. They might be compared to parish curates in that they have only the authority and responsibility assigned by the bishop. They can do only what is assigned to them, and their responsibilities, unlike those of coadjutors, may be changed on the order of the bishop. Suffragans have no automatic right to succession. Some have been elected to diocesan posts, but many have remained in office to serve a succession of diocesan bishops.

All bishops may be elected to a diocese other than the one they are currently serving, although a diocesan has to serve at least five years in the first post before being eligible for election to another diocese. This means, in effect, that a bishop need not feel that election to a particular diocesan post is for life, or until the mandatory retirement age of 72.

Diocesan bishops operate with equal authority and are theoretically independent of one another. In practice, however, they have relinquished certain authority to two national bodies: the House of Bishops and the General Convention. The General Convention is composed of the House of Bishops and the House of Deputies. The bishops meet annually and have certain authority during the years between conventions. Since some authority has been relinquished, diocesan canon law has to agree with national canon law, although there might be local canons with no application nationally.

The General Convention meets triennially, with the possibility of special conventions being called by the presiding bishop if there is some business that cannot wait for three years. This has happened twice, in 1831 and 1969. In 1973 the canon was changed and the word "triennial" was dropped in favor of "regular." This gives Convention the opportunity to set the next date if it chooses to meet again in less than three years.

The House of Deputies is made up of an equal number of clergy and lay deputies: four from each diocese. It is not a representative body and the deputies for the most part go to Convention uninstructed. They do not go as diocesan delegates obliged to vote in a particular way. Deputies and an equal number of alternates are elected by diocesan conventions. In 1970 General Convention voted to seat women deputies, a proposition that had come before it for more than twenty years.

The two houses elect their own officers. The presiding bishop serves as chairman of the House of Bishops, which also elects a vice-chairman and a secretary. The House of Deputies elects a president, vice-president, and secretary. The secretary is an administrative officer who serves during the years between conventions. The president appoints chairmen or chairwomen as well as the members of committees. These are the real work groups of the Convention and the appointments are important. Most of the committees have open hearings on resolutions, and much of the important debate and reworking of legislation takes place at these hearings.

Dioceses are assessed for the expenses of the Convention with a "head tax" based on the number of clergy who are canonically resident within the diocese. Most dioceses also pay the expenses of deputies attending the Convention. There are about 1,000 bishops and deputies in attendance, and some 18,000 people may take part in the ten-day deliberations, making it one of the largest conventions meeting in the United States.

The General Convention is the supreme policy-making body of the Episcopal Church. It includes both bishops and deputies, since all legislation requires the concurrence of both houses. Convention not only sets the budget and program for the Church, but also determines mission strategy, revises the constitution and canons, and conducts other business. All voting is by a simple majority on substantive issues, although a vote "by orders" may be called by the clerical or lay deputations of 3 dioceses. This means that lay and clergy deputies vote separately, with each deputation of four receiving one recorded vote. If the deputation is split 2-2, it has the effect of being cast in the negative, as a measure can pass in a vote "by orders" only if the "yes" votes outnumber others by at least one and if the vote in both clergy and lay orders concur in that majority. Some important legislation has failed to pass when a vote "by orders" has been used. In 1970 and in 1973, for example, the majority of the deputies on the floor voted in favor of ordaining women to the priesthood, but on both occasions the vote "by orders" resulted in the defeat of the proposal.

Whenever the office of the presiding bishop becomes vacant the House of Bishops votes for a new presiding officer with the House of Deputies concurring. It is clearly an election by the bishops, who are choosing their chairman and chief pastor as well as the chief officer of the Church. Clerical and lay deputies traditionally have no direct influence on the matter, but in 1973 there were clerical and lay deputies as well as bishops on the nominating committee appointed to fill the vacancy to be created by the resignation of the Rt. Rev. John E. Hines in 1974.

The presiding bishop has no extra authority in the Episcopal Church, but shares authority with every other bishop. By the nature of his office, however, he has certain honors and he speaks from an honored position clearly identifying him with the Church. He is a first among equals and is a spokesman for the Episcopal Church. He is elected from the membership of the House of Bishops and is the chief consecrator at most Episcopal consecrations and the chief administrative officer of the national headquarters. His term of office is limited to 12 years, or until he reaches 65 years of age.

In the period between conventions Church policy is carried out by the Executive Council. This central body is made up of 20 members elected by General Convention and 2 members from each of the nine provincial synods. The presiding bishop is the chairman and is an ex officio member, as is the president of the House of Deputies. The 20 members elected by General Convention include 4 bishops, 4 presbyters, and 12 lay members. These, together with provincial members, help keep the Executive Council representative of the Church by orders and geography. Executive Council revises the budget annually to meet changes in income and expenses, thus setting some policy in its own right. It approves missionary appointments and it, too, speaks with a certain authority. Executive Council resolutions, although usually carrying a disclaimer from being the voice of the Church, are often regarded as such.

Aside from the official Church structure, there exists an organization of women, the Episcopal Church Women (ECW), which enjoys power and prestige nationally, as well as on diocesan and local levels. The ECW used to elect representatives to Executive Council, but that procedure ended in 1970 when women were seated as deputies in General Convention and became eligible for election to decision-making positions.

The growth of the status of women in the Episcopal

Church has coincided with their growth in American culture. Prior to the 1960s women could not serve on vestries, as delegates to most diocesan conventions, or in General Convention. In the 1960s there was a strong thrust to change diocesan and national constitutions and canons to enrich the life of the Church by bringing in women on all levels of lay leadership. Plans were in progress to end the ECW as a separate organization. This had been done in the Anglican Church of Canada and in certain parishes, provincial synods, and dioceses in the United States. But in 1973 the membership of the ECW voted to continue as a separate organization.

The Episcopal Church Women continues to meet triennially, with about 600 representatives, including, since 1967, at least one man. They meet at the same time and in the same place as General Convention. One of the most important works of the ECW is the allocation of funds raised by the United Thank Offering (UTO). This has been a practice of long tradition, originally carried out by the Women's Auxiliary (See Chapter 1). UTO is symbolized by blue mite boxes in the homes of many Episcopalians. Coins are placed in the boxes in thanksgiving and to commemorate family life. The coins are offered through parishes, then dioceses, and then at the triennial meeting where the UTO collection is celebrated with a festive Eucharist. The offering has amounted to over one million dollars a year and has been used for needs at home and abroad.

# 4

# LITURGY

THE Eucharist was the principal liturgical act of the Church for the first 1,000 years of its history. Christians consider that Christ instituted the sacrament with these words:

> Jesus replied, "In truth, in very truth I tell you, unless you eat the flesh of the Son of Man and drink his blood you can have no life in you. Whoever eats my flesh and drinks my blood possesses eternal life, and I will raise him up on the last day. My flesh is real food; my blood is real drink. Whoever eats my flesh and drinks my blood dwells continually in me and I dwell in him. As the living Father sent me, and I live because of the Father, so he who eats me shall live because of the Father, so he who eats me shall live because of me. This is the bread which came

down from heaven; and it is not like the bread which our fathers ate; they are dead, but whoever eats this bread shall live forever" (Jn. 6:53–58).

St. Paul passed the tradition on to the Christians at Corinth in these words:

> For the tradition which I handed on to you came to me from the Lord himself: that the Lord Jesus, on the night of his arrest, took bread and after giving thanks to God, broke it and said: "This is my body, which is for you; do this as a memorial of me." In the same way, he took the cup after supper, and said: "This cup is the new covenant sealed by my blood. Whenever you drink it, do this as a memorial of me." For every time you eat this bread and drink this cup, you proclaim the death of the Lord, until he comes (1 Cor. 11:23–26).

The Eucharist, also known as the Holy Communion and the Liturgy of the Lord's Supper, occupies the central place in the theology of the Episcopal Church. All forms of liturgical worship in the Book of Common Prayer extend from the Eucharist. Even though some may be used independently, the Prayer Book presumes that when the Body of Christ is gathered, its members will break bread and share wine from the common cup. Communion is one of the two sacraments (the other being Baptism) that has been traditionally regarded as generally necessary for salvation.

Although the Prayer Book Catechism takes a sacramental view of other major liturgical acts of the Church, the Articles of Religion (the Thirty-nine Articles) found in the Prayer Book treat them separately. These are Confirmation, Marriage, Ordination, Penance, and Unction. Article XXV, although not binding, has guided the Church's thinking on the matter since the articles were promulgated in the 16th century. The five cannot be said to have been ordained by Christ, nor are they possible of practice by everyone. Hence, they are not "sacraments of the Gospel."

The word *liturgy* finds its derivation in the Greek word *leitourgia* which is put together from *laos* (people), and *ergon* (work). Thus liturgy is the work of the people and for the people. It is best used to describe municipal services, the public works that are necessary for the community. *Worship* also finds its roots in the old English word *werk*. When liturgy is applied to the sacramental acts of the Church, it carries with it the strong implication of work, or worship, of the people. The sacraments are for the people, to be engaged in by the people, and celebrated by the people under the leadership of a priest who serves as president at the Communion meal and as chief officer at other liturgical acts.

Although throughout history the Church has gone through certain purges and excesses, the sacrament of the Eucharist has emergel in its simplicity as the central act of worship. The Reformation attempted to purge the excesses by restoring worship to the people, who had become so priest-ridden that they were, by and large, excluded from receiving the elements and reduced to watching as the priests communicated. The sacraments had become too "holy" for the common folk. Even church architecture divided the people from the priests with a rood screen between sanctuary and nave. Bells were used to awaken the people at the time of the Sanctus and Consecration so that they could dutifully kneel and be pious, even though they often could not see what was going on.

At the same time, the Reformation attempted to rid the celebrations of undue mysticism centered on many saints and Masses for the dead. Particularly objectionable was the practice of selling indulgences to the common people "enabling" them to "earn" favor in heaven by attendance at Masses, or by performing certain acts of penance.

The result of the struggles of reformation and renewal has been to emphasize that the Eucharist is for the people—the chief act of the Church, available to the commonest of people and to the greatest.

At the heart of the Eucharist is the *anamnesis,* a Greek word that has been translated as *memorial.* Its meaning is far deeper than the idea of memorializing an event, which is a general Protestant interpretation of Communion. *Anamnesis* means to recall—to call into the present the events of the past in order to relive those events.

The whole of Jesus' life, death, and resurrection are recalled at the Eucharist and appropriated by the participants to be lived anew as each life is made new in the reception of the body and blood of our Lord. This is indeed a different approach from doing something because it was done before, or doing something to provoke a memory.

The theme of the oneness of the people who receive and the Christ who gives is contained in all of the alternative forms of the prayer of consecration, or Great Thanksgiving. One specifically uses the words, "that we and all thy whole Church may be made one body with him, that he may dwell in us, and we in him." Thus the president of the meal recognizes that the faithful of God gathered at his table *are* the Body of Christ, strengthened and made righteous and put on mission.

The Eucharistic office, Morning Prayer, Evening Prayer, and the other offices of the Episcopal Church are collected in the Book of Common Prayer. The Prayer Book contains all services necessary for fulfillment of the religious life of man from birth (baptism) to death (burial). It is a book that has been and is being continually revised to meet the exigencies of the day. Thus, although it contains many ancient prayers and practices, it also reflects contemporary language and forms. And it maintains a worship structure that dates, in some ways, to the pre-Christian practices of the synagogues of the diaspora—the time of the dispersion of the Jews after the Babylonian exile. The Preface to the Prayer Book anticipates continual change and revision to meet the needs of the time. The Prayer Book is also a unifying force within Anglicanism. Every national, independent Church in the Anglican Communion has its own Prayer Book with vernacular worship, often reflecting cultural practices of the region. Yet all can find a relationship to the revisions as they flowed from England. Episcopalians, therefore, can find some continuity wherever they might worship in the Anglican Communion, regardless of language differences.

As the Church in the turbulent times of the 16th and 17th centuries vacillated between Catholic and Protestant influences, subsequent Prayer Books reflected the theology of the times. The *Second Prayer Book of Edward VI* was little used because of Edward's early death in 1553. Queen Mary restored the Latin Service Books, but in the reign of Elizabeth I, the Prayer Book was reissued in English and was revised variously until 1662. This 1662 Prayer Book is the official Prayer Book of the Church of England and is still used in other parts of the Anglican Communion. It is the one that served as a model for most of the Prayer Books which developed as the Anglican Communion developed.

This is the Prayer Book that was brought to the American colonies by early explorers and used until 1789 when, at the General Convention of the American Church in Philadelphia, the first American Prayer Book was published. It was a revision of the 1662 version, but with the important addition of the Communion consecration prayer from the Scottish Prayer Book. The Scottish book was influenced by Eastern Orthodoxy and so the American Prayer Book has merged the Western and Eastern traditions in the Eucharistic liturgy. The American Prayer Book has been revised several times, with major changes being made in 1892 and 1928 and 1976. The 1979 revision, containing both traditional and contemporary language and service forms, was the result of nearly twelve years of testing of trial rites. It was the first Prayer Book that reflected the growth of liturgy from the people whose opinions were requested by the Standing Liturgical Commission as it completed the revision.

When one speaks of the Prayer Book today, one is probably referring to a way of worship, an order, rather than to a specific edition of the Book of Common Prayer. Although the revision of 1928 is likely to be found in some Episcopal Church pews as a symbol of a strong heritage from the past, the 1979 revision continues that heritage and liturgical order and will become the usual book until some other revision takes place.

The Prayer Book has never dictated uniformity of worship. A newcomer to the Episcopal Church could find different ceremonial practices in different churches, and could be put off either by the enrichment of ceremony or a dearth of it, depending on one's background and expectations. Still the order remains constant. But a person born and reared in a single congregation could be put off equally because of the differences inherent in the universal Anglican Communion.

The order of worship does not vary a great deal throughout the Anglican Communion. One prayer leads to another; the Creed comes at approximately the same time and place; the Lord's Prayer is a highlight of every service. Unlike the old Roman Catholic Latin rite which ensured that a Roman Catholic would find the same Mass said throughout the world, the Episcopalian will find each Anglican church to be somewhat different, reflecting its own cultural and national heritage. In fact, each Episcopal parish church reflects a unique congregational tradition that sets it apart from the rest.

The Daily Office of Morning and Evening Prayer with which the Prayer Book begins is supplementary to the sacrament of Holy Communion. It is a prayer office surrounding the reading of Scripture and the recitation of Psalms. It is monastic in conception, combining as it does the eight Divine Offices into two.

The eight hours, kept as a preparation for the Eucharist in monasteries, consisted of the night office of Matins, and the day hours of Lauds, Prime, Terce, Sext, None, Vespers, and Compline. During the years of intense reaction to Roman Catholicism, beginning with Edward VI and continuing through the Elizabethan Settlement to the present day, many parishes adopted the Daily Office as their principal Sunday services, relegating the Eucharist to an early morning celebration, and once a month as the major service of the day. In fact, there were times when the Eucharist was celebrated quarterly, especially during the years of Puritan influence.

Morning and Evening Prayer are corporate in scope, and work best when said daily by groups that already share a common life, such as religious orders, schools, or communes. Although some priests and lay persons have a discipline of saying the Daily Office, it has fallen into disuse as a daily congregational expression in most parishes. When the Daily Office is followed in a disciplined manner, the Bible will be read in a two-year cycle, and the 150 psalms will be read in a seven-week cycle. As congregations have responded to the liturgical movement, restoring the centrality of the Eucharist to parish life, Morning Prayer has sometimes been used in its brief form, allowing for the Scripture reading and a few prayers as ante-Communion (the Ministry of the Word).

The centrality of the Eucharist focuses on membership in the Church as well as discipline. A communicant of the Episcopal Church is a person who is confirmed, who is duly enrolled in a congregation and who regularly receives Communion. Legally, to remain a communicant, a person should receive Holy Communion three times a year, but the Prayer Book presumes a weekly observance of the Eucharist.

Since the Church administers Communion to unconfirmed persons who have been baptized, the stringency of the requirement of Confirmation is not what it once was. A person who wants to affiliate fully with the Episcopal Church will want to receive Confirmation —the laying-on-of-hands by the bishop—not only as a sacrament but as a means of reaffirming baptismal vows. This Confirmation is not only a part of the initiation rite to be coupled with Baptism; it is also a rite of passage providing for the affirmation of faith in a mature setting. Until the Church provides another rite through which a person may acknowledge his or her faith as a mature expression of commitment and willingness to submit to the discipline of the Christian Church, it will continue to hold Confirmation separate from Baptism.

In the early days of the Church, Christian initiation —Baptism and Confirmation—was regarded as one act to be followed immediately by Holy Communion. People received instruction for two or three years. On Easter Eve they gathered for the Easter Vigil and for initiation. Whole families are thought to have been initiated, giving justification to the practice of infant Baptism. Initiation included Baptism, the laying-on-of-hands by the bishop, the use of chrism or blessed oil, and Communion.

Baptism, then, is the chief rite of initiation into the Christian religion, hence into the Church. A baptized person is considered to be a member of the Church, having fully received the Holy Spirit in the mystical act of being buried (immersed), cleansed of sin, and resurrected to live with Christ. Baptism, although a washing away of sins, also anticipates that the person so initiated will have a new life, with the possibility of living always within the direction of the Holy Spirit, nurtured through the Church to practice Christianity and to realize its joys and strengths. Baptism is the opportunity for new life, cleansed of sin, in a community of persons also committed to making that life possible.

The idea of Baptism *in extremis,* or rushing the infant to the font within eight days for fear he or she might die and remain in limbo, is a later medieval addition to Christian theology. Many parishes today are setting aside particular Sundays for Baptism; some are returning to the traditional Easter and Pentecost dates. Most are recognizing the corporate nature of Baptism and are not practicing private Baptisms. The whole point is for the family (congregation) to be there to welcome its new member. Private Baptisms exclude the wider family and too often have been done primarily as preludes to private parties. Baptisms should be great celebrations open to all those responsible for the nurture of the new member. Only in extreme situations, such as illness, should Baptism be done privately.

Until 1970, children and adults who had not been confirmed were not expected to receive Communion in the Episcopal Church. A medieval rubric found in older prayer books reads: "And there shall none be admitted to the Holy Communion, until such time as he be confirmed, or be ready and desirous to be confirmed." The rubric was intended as an instruction to bishops to be diligent about Confirmation. It has been removed from the 1979 revision, recognizing that it is a matter of discipline and not theology. But some priests continue to require confirmation before communion in their parishes. Some confusion naturally developed as the Church had more ecumenical involvements and as more non-Episcopalians were visiting Episcopal churches. Many were used to receiving Communion in their own churches and were offended at the idea of closed Communion. Some priests communicated them without any concern; others wanted legal justification for doing so; some refused on any account as they were committed to the literal interpretation of the rubric. Some dioceses had been for some time openly inviting visitors to the altar, but at the same time excluding their own children because they were not confirmed. This created ambiguity that was difficult to justify. It placed a great deal of weight on intellectual understanding before receiving, whereas the argument could be offered that Communion is a mystery and a gift of God rather than a sacrament of intellectual understanding.

Theologically, since there is no dogma, such diversity is possible in the Episcopal Church. The Church has practiced, along with all of Anglicanism, a *via media,* a middle way. For some it is too accepting and makes them uncomfortable; others find that its insistence on some practices of belief, as summed up in the Nicene Creed, is too restrictive. Nevertheless, the Episcopal Church teaches that the Nicene Creed contains the basic affirmations of Christian belief and that Episcopalians should accede to them. The Nicene Creed is said at the major celebrations of the Holy Eucharist; and the Baptismal Creed, which is the Apostles' Creed, is said at every recitation of the Daily Office.

The Church has not set down a strict interpretation of the creedal statement, so there is room within it for continuing growth in understanding as well as interpretation. There are members of the Episcopal Church who are biblical fundamentalists and give literal interpretation to the Creed. There are also persons who reject almost all forms of fundamentalism or supernaturalism; and they, too, can find a way of reciting the Creed with integrity. This means that references to the Virgin Birth and the bodily resurrection of Jesus are open to interpretation without a dogmatic requirement by the Church for a specific belief, or a condemnation for an inability to believe. People who cannot accept these acts as biologically possible can deal with them on a figurative level as expressions of the mystery of God, whose actions cannot always be explained but are always open for exploration and attempts at explanation. The Creed, in fact, attempts to explain the mighty acts of God in one statement. It has withstood the test of centuries as the best possible statement the Church could make. The International Consultation on English Texts, agreed upon by Roman Catholics, Lutherans, Anglicans, and others, has also restored the ancient and plural "we" for the "I" before "believe." The Creed is felt to be a recitation of the belief of the Church corporate rather than (necessarily) the belief of the individual. Statements in the Creed that cannot be held literally by an individual can be supported as expressions of the faith of the whole Church, recognizing the vast differences of individual theological understanding and interpretation.

Just as the Episcopal Church has not required a particular dogmatic interpretation of the Creed, it has not provided a particular dogmatic explanation of the Real Presence of Christ in the Eucharist. The Church does believe that Christ is really present with his people when they gather at his table to break bread and to share his body and blood in the way he instituted at the Last Supper. The Thirty-nine Articles, finally approved in 1571 by Convocation of the Church of England, were an attempt to give short, dogmatic interpretations of the Church's position on controversies which raged in the 16th Century. Thus the Articles counter some of the theological assertions of the Council of Trent as well as certain Protestant doctrines growing out of Zwinglianism and Calvinism in Geneva. Although the Thirty-nine Articles are deemed important enough to be printed as part of the Book of Common Prayer, their subscription has not been required. They serve as possible guidance, but they have no authority.

Article XXVIII warns against a belief in transubstantiation. But there are Episcopalians who believe in transubstantiation: that the bread and wine actually become the body and blood of Christ at the time of consecration. Another view is receptionism which rejects the idea that the elements themselves change but holds that the Real Presence is in the faith of the communicant in the reception of the elements.

Undoubtedly there are Episcopalians who hold to none of those views, but who take a Protestant position that the meal is a memory-provoker, or an act of the Church in which they participate out of a sense of discipline or acceptance of its symbolic qualities emphasizing the corporate nature of humankind.

The Church has no firm theology or dogma which tells the people exactly what they must believe. Episcopalians are taught that scripture contains all things necessary for salvation and scripture has from its beginning been open to interpretation. Nor has the Church required any set ceremony for performing any service. The rubrics are quite general and, with renewal in liturgical practices becoming the norm in most congregations, they can be confusing if followed to the letter.

The lack of instruction means that ceremony itself will be different from congregation to congregation. This has caused some uncertainty for people as they visit new parishes or move into new communities. It might be noted that there is no theological justification for physical worship on the part of the people; whether they sign themselves in the name of the Trinity; genuflect, bow, or do nothing to acknowledge either the reserved Sacrament or the altar. One of the old, rather romantic messages that one can still find in some church bulletins says: "We kneel to pray, stand to praise, and sit to learn." Yet one can find people standing to pray in many churches. In the ancient churches, the people stood most of the time as they gathered in bare rooms kneeling only for certain prayers on fast days. It was only after the Reformation, when preaching became so important and lasted so long, that benches were brought into the church.

People may kneel or stand to receive Communion, and some churches have provided for that contingency by removing altar rails and opening the chancel. Some people may choose to *intinct* (dip the bread into the wine) rather than share the common cup, either out of some feeling about drinking after another person or because they have an ailment, such as a cold, which they feel might be contagious. There has been no record of disease being passed through the sharing of the cup. If the risks were great, most priests would be quite ill most of the time as they usually consume what is left over. Intinction dates to the seventh century, but as Communion became more and more a practice of the clergy, the chalice was removed altogether from the people, who, if they received at all, received only in one kind—the bread. The chalice was restored to common worship after the English Reformation.

The ceremony in some churches is simple; in others, very elaborate, and there are many gradations between. In some, the priest will conduct the service dressed in Victorian garments: black cassock, white surplice, and black tippet or shawl, changing to a stole for Communion. In another the priest will use the Eucharistic garment, the chasuble, and a deacon and subdeacon (a lay person) will be dressed in matching dalmatic and tunicle. One church may have votive candles burning in front of a cross in a side chapel, or a statue of the Virgin Mary. Another may use candles sparingly, even on the altar, with no statues or crucifixes in view. One congregation might use incense and great liturgical processions for the Gospel readings. They may process around the church when the Litany is said or sung, or on great festival days such as Easter and Christmas. Another might have only a choir procession behind a simple cross at the beginning of the service. No matter what the arrangement of services might be— and some are directly related to the size and wealth of the congregation—the words or ritual of the services will be basically the same.

In liturgy, as in much of its religious expression, the Episcopal Church seeks the *via media*, retaining access to its strong tradition but allowing for fresh approaches in God's continuing creative relationship with his people.

# 5

# THE LAY MINISTRY

EVERY Christian is expected to be a missionary. The promises given at Baptism are an assurance that the new Christian will take his stand with other Christians through the centuries to proclaim the "Good News." Baptism is therefore an ordination to mission. As the individual is brought into the midst of the family of God for the initiation, he is presented to the assembled family to be nurtured in Christian knowledge and life. At the same time, the new member joins the family to witness to the Christian life by act as well as by voice. Thus, the mission of the Church is as much in the hands of the laity as in the hands of the clergy.

It is a mistake to regard the clergy as the missionaries primarily responsible for bringing people to the Church. Almost anyone who has joined the Church as an adult will recall that it was a lay person who first brought him into the congregation. The style of worship or a particular clergyman may contribute to an individual's decision to join the Church, either transferring from another Christian body or changing from a nonbaptized state. In the majority of cases, the primary influence has been that of another lay person.

There are many ways a lay person may exercise his ministry. The Church stands ready to encourage ministry with adult education and training methods. Clergy and lay counselors are available to help guide those ministries into effective channels. It is not necessary to be an expert in theology. Contact with another person about his relationship with Jesus is far more impressive than the theology of that relationship. Simple witness to one's own life in Christ means more than the theology approved by Church authority.

Witnessing includes doing the will of God, serving. It means caring for others and helping them, and it is as incumbent on the Church to be a servant as it is on the individual. The lay person who works and lives on this level will discover that if he is acting in concert with other parish members, the congregation itself will evidence a truly corporate life. Such a congregation will grow much as the first Church in Jerusalem grew. We learn from the Book of Acts (2:46–47):

> With one mind they kept up their daily attendance at the temple, and breaking bread in private houses, shared their meals with unaffected joy, as they praised God and enjoyed the favour of the whole people. And day by day the Lord added to their number those whom he was saving.

It can be expected that God will give the increase to congregations that evidence wholesome, serving aspects of the Christian community. This requires a strong sense of commitment on the part of the members and a resolution to live the Christian life. Although the most effective lay mission will be conducted by the particular lay person alongside his fellow man at work or within a social context, there are also lay jobs in the Church which are dependent upon volunteers.

One such job is that of the lay reader, an office licensed by the bishop of the diocese. A lay reader may take charge of small congregations, usually mission churches that are without the regular ministration of a priest. If the bishop gives permission, lay readers may preach their own sermons. Otherwise they read prepared sermons written specifically for lay presentation. They may read the Daily Office and conduct funerals; they may visit the sick and infirm. When licensed to do so, they may administer the chalice during Holy Communion.

Canon III. 26.2 requires that an applicant for a lay reader's license be regular in attendance and active in support of the parish. It also provides that a lay reader who is assigned pastoral or administrative responsibilities be trained and examined in such subjects as the Bible, the Prayer Book and Hymnal, Church history, the Church's doctrine, the conduct of worship, and pastoral care. This requirement for training has given rise to lay schools of theology in many dioceses, which lay persons must attend before they are licensed. Licensing certain persons as lay readers does not restrict the participation of other laity. Some parishes rotate the responsibilities of reading among any of the laity who are willing to participate.

If the laity are to perform duties within the Church, exercising a lay mission, they should be well-informed about the Church itself, the Creeds, and the Scriptures. One way for a person to learn about the Church is to read one or more of its periodicals. Almost every diocese has a publication—newspaper or magazine. The total circulation of these periodicals indicates that almost every Episcopal family receives Church literature.

An informed lay person will also want to read in theology and might find the *Anglican Theological Review* helpful. There are good ecumenical magazines: the liberal *Christian Century* and the more conservative *Christianity Today*. Other valuable periodicals are the *National Catholic Reporter* and *Commonweal*. Although designed specifically for Roman Catholic readership, their articles are highly interesting and informative for all Christians. Those interested in Church history might want to read the *Historical Magazine*, a quarterly published by the Church Historical Society (Austin, Texas).

There is no reason for a lay person to be ignorant of Bible content. The Prayer Book lectionary, if followed daily, will provide an almost complete reading of the Bible every two years. The new ecumenical lectionary provides a three-year cycle of Sunday readings. The Prayer Book is highly scriptural in content and has a specific provision for family prayer to encourage daily devotions by members of the Church. If families or individuals discipline themselves to daily prayer, Bible reading is easy; if they attend Church regularly, they will hear large portions of the Bible and sermons relating Scripture to daily life.

There is a disciplined way of life for the lay person in the Church. Rubrics in the Book of Common Prayer give a great deal of direction for Church discipline, and other matters can be found in Canon Law. (The Canons are available from the national headquarters or from the Seabury Press.) Discipline does not mean a lack of freedom. Rather, it provides a framework of order for Church members. Most of the Church's discipline is centered in Holy Communion, and the greatest penalty the Church can impose is excommunication, which prohibits a member from receiving Holy Communion. This is not a light matter and the priest does not excommunicate without good cause, or without giving an individual a chance to appeal the ruling to the bishop. Therefore, the concept of excommunication presumes a deep sense of commitment by the person on whom it is imposed. Regular church attendance and communication is a voluntary matter to begin with. Acts worthy of excommunication have to be overt and an offense to the whole community, not individual sins that can be dealt with pastorally by the priest. There is a procedure for restoring those excommunicated.

Church attendance is a matter of discipline, and regular communication is expected of Church members on Sundays. The Prayer Book makes this clear in the Catechism (p. 856)

*Question:* What is the duty of all Christians?

*Answer:* The duty of all Christians is to follow Christ; to come together week by week for corporate worship; and to work, pray, and give for the spread of the kingdom of God.

The Canon, "Of the Due Celebration of Sundays,"
(II.1) also makes this clear:

> All persons within this Church shall celebrate and
> keep the Lord's Day, commonly called Sunday, by
> regular participation in the public worship of the
> Church, by hearing the Word of God read and
> taught, and by other acts of devotion and works of
> Charity, using all godly and other conversation.

The Canon amplifies this discipline with requirements for being a member in good standing. Canon I.16
points out:

> All baptized persons who shall for one year next
> preceding have fulfilled the requirements of the
> Canon, "Of the Due Celebration of Sundays" unless
> for good cause prevented, are members of this
> Church in good standing.

To be a communicant in good standing, one has to
fulfill those expectations and receive Confirmation by a
bishop of the Episcopal Church (or have been received
by a bishop from another Catholic Church) and also
"unless for good cause prevented, have received Holy
Communion at least thrice during the next preceding
year . . ." The Canon contemplated the traditional
requirement of Communion at Christmas and Easter, and
at least one other time during the year. This seems to
contradict the requirement of regular public worship,
with the Eucharist as the central act of the Church,
because, conceivably, a person could receive three Sun-

days in a row and fulfill the requirements. In this case, the Church apparently wishes to use these regulations as guidelines.

The Church also expects every member to carry his fair share of the financial burden. The response to the question about one's Christian duty is answered not only by the responsibility to worship, but also by the clear command "to work, pray, and give for the spread of the kingdom of God."

Also, pledging to the Church is a voluntary act and is considered to be an agreement between the Church member and God. It has been traditionally acknowledged that the pledger should consider tithing as a guideline for giving. The biblical tithe is ten percent of income. Jesus carried giving beyond that with the requirement that one give himself totally to the work of the Kingdom. This can be illustrated by the story of the poor widow:

> Once he was standing opposite the temple treasury, watching as people dropped their money into the chest. Many rich people were giving large sums. Presently there came a poor widow who dropped in two tiny coins, together worth a farthing. He called his disciples to him. "I tell you this," he said: "this poor widow has given more than any of the others; for those others who have given had more than enough, but she, with less than enough, has given all that she had to live on" (Mark 12:41–44).

Christian stewardship draws from the teaching of Jesus, the giving of a totality of life, a sacrificial response to spreading the Kingdom. The office does not spell out what is meant by working for the Kingdom, but it can be considered that living a Christian life morally and ethically based on the commandment to love God, neighbor, and self would be working for the Kingdom. It can also be considered that a true response to the realization that all things come from God and are to be returned to him allows a person to place his dependence on God and not on material things, and to utilize the material benefits to support Church and charity.

Giving is a concrete proposition. In a money economy, money is representative of one's life and labor. It is money that God gives, and this is to be shared for the furtherance of the work of the Church, its mission rather than its institutional preservation. Some people try to tithe, sharing a percentage of their income with the Church and a percentage with secular, charitable organizations that they believe to be dealing with the human condition. Others feel that tithing means giving a total of ten percent to the Church and that any other money for charity should be in addition to that.

Stewardship is not a matter of legalistic sharing of income, but pertains to the totality of one's care of God's world. Church giving can symbolize that care. The Church has taught sacrificial giving.

The Church is usually quite considerate of people who cannot and do not make pledges. Most pledge cards have a notation that at any time the person wants to increase or decrease his pledge, he need only see the treasurer and tell him. This is a private matter, and no questions are asked. But a pledge is a moral obligation and should be paid just as any other bill is paid; first of all, in recognition of the importance of the God-man relationship it symbolizes.

One of the best ways for a person to decide on the stewardship of money is to follow the biblical idea of offering the first fruits to God. This is an old and honored tradition. When the first fruits were actually the fruits of the harvest, or the first-born of animal herds, the first was considered the best and was taken to the Temple, offered to God, and given over. Budgets can easily be drawn so that the pledge is at the top of the budget and the rest of the budget is based on what is left over.

Church members are also under discipline with regard to children they present for baptism, whether as parents or godparents. In the baptismal service such persons solemnly promise to bring the child up in the Christian faith and life. A rubric on page 298 of the Prayer Book states: "Parents and godparents are to be instructed in the meaning of Baptism, in their duties to help the new Christians grow in the knowledge and love of God, and in their responsibilities as members of his Church."

Perhaps the firmest discipline applied by the Church has been in the most personal life of its members in the relationship of marriage. Two entire canons are devoted to Holy Matrimony, and until November 1, 1973, they were most stringently applicable to persons seeking to be married after divorces. The complicated rules of the past amounted to an annulment procedure requiring the submission of all materials, including the divorce decree, to the bishop of the diocese in which the marriage was to be performed. If the bishop agreed, sometimes with the judgment rendered by an appointed marriage court of priests, then the marriage could take place. At least a year had to elapse after a divorce before an application for remarriage could be submitted.

But the General Convention in 1973 put an end to that procedure with a virtual rewrite of Canons I.17 and I.18 providing a greater pastoral role for the priest, replacing the set of legal rules which seemed more designed to turn people away from the Church than to reach out to them in love and concern. The new Canon has pastoral and other regulations which both the minister and the persons who intend to marry each other have to agree upon. One section, which is of long standing, gives the minister the discretion to decline to solemnize any marriage.

Persons desiring the rite of matrimony in the Church have to make their wishes known at least 30 days before the service, unless there is a satisfactory reason for not doing so.

The big change has been made in Canon I.18, entitled "Of Regulations Respecting Holy Matrimony: Concerning Preservation of Marriage, Dissolution of Marriage, and Remarriage." The ratio of divorces to marriages has been on an increase in this country for a long time, and only in 1973 did the Church begin to deal with it creatively by recognizing the fact and providing a means for divorced people to remain communicants after remarriage. Until this change people who did not seek the Church's counsel on divorce often fared better than those submitting themselves to the discipline.

When marriages are in trouble, the canon says that it is the duty of either or both parties to consult a "Minister of this Church" before contemplating legal action, and the minister is instructed to work to effect a reconciliation. However, if a member's marriage has been annulled or dissolved by civil action, the bishop may be asked for a judgment, which may be "a recognition of the nullity, or of the termination of the said marriage." That judgment becomes part of the permanent record of the diocese.

The Canon then provides regulations for the minister to adhere to before solemnizing a marriage of a divorced person whose former spouse is still living, or before a member of the Church can be married if either of the contracting parties has a former spouse still living. These all extend the pastoral role of the minister.

First the minister must have evidence that the prior marriage was annulled or dissolved by a final judgment or decree of a civil court. Then the parties must be made aware of the need for continuing concern for the well-being of the former spouse and the children, if any, of the prior marriage. The minister then consults with the bishop for consent to solemnize the marriage, and after the ceremony, reports to the bishop that it was performed. If one bishop consents, but the wedding is performed in another diocese, then the bishop of the new jurisdiction must have affirmed the consent before the marriage could take place.

There are members of the Church who have been virtually ignorant of the Church's stand on marriage and divorce, but there have been others who have loyally acceded to those regulations and who have subsequently been excommunicated, some moving to other denominations, some dropping out of participation in the Christian Church altogether. It is hoped that those people can seek the Church's blessing on their new unions in light of the new canons. The Church has an office for the blessing of marriages performed civilly, and most priests are interested in helping people find fulfillment through the life of the Church by enabling them to receive its sacraments and to enjoy its community through such blessings.

In order to maintain good relationships with congregations, especially within a mobile society, the Church has a regular form of transferring enrollments, and members are expected to transfer when they move. (Canon I.16:5) Membership is primarily in the Episcopal Church and secondarily in a congregation. The clergy are quite anxious to do the necessary paper work so that the Church members can affiliate quickly with a new community and receive the ministrations of the new body. The Church is often the first place people can take their personal problems, and membership in the local body encourages them to turn to the local minister when there are personal troubles in their lives.

At the same time, members should take their membership seriously and try to give as much of themselves in the parish as they can. There are important lay positions in the decision-making bodies of a parish: the vestry, the parish council, and other groups. Lay persons can also serve at the diocesan level. The diocesan convention, the most important policy-making body on the diocesan level, will have lay representatives from each parish. It would be helpful if Church members tried to elect committed members to represent their congregations so that office-holding does not become a matter of convenience rather than concern.

The Church is dependent on the laity to serve as teachers, and it seems that only a few parishes ever have an adequate Church School faculty. Priests are often reluctant to ask professional teachers, who are in classrooms all week, to teach also on Sunday. So, teaching in church often becomes a training process in itself. Some people have discovered a special talent when they have taught for the first time.

For lay persons who wish to give more of themselves in some sort of full-time Church work there is the Church Army. This organization was started in 1882 in London, and its work has been similar to that of the Salvation Army. Workers are commissioned as captains or sisters, and most of them work in poverty programs of the inner city, on Indian reservations, or in relatively remote areas of the country. The Church Army has had its ups and downs in the United States, and it has never been very large here. Where its people have been working, however, it has been very effective.

Many of the religious orders also admit lay members who serve a novitiate before being cloaked as brothers or sisters. They may be professed for life. Others who are interested in developing a disciplined prayer life can become associates in the orders. Rules developed by the orders for their associates usually require some sort of daily devotions and meditations, regular Communions, and sometimes an annual retreat.

# 6

# THE ORDAINED MINISTRY

THE Preface to the Ordination rites in the Book of Common Prayer explains the ministry of the Episcopal Church. It has its roots in the earlier Prayer Books of the Church of England and envisions an apostolic concept of the ministry. It refers to the rites of ordination of bishops, priests, and deacons, and the Preface says (page 510) in part:

> The Holy Scriptures and ancient Christian writers make it clear that from the apostles' time, there have been different ministries within the Church. In particular, since the time of the New Testament, three distinct orders of ordained ministers have been characteristic of Christ's holy catholic Church. . . . The persons who are chosen and recognized by the Church as being called by God

to the ordained ministry are admitted to these sacred orders by solemn prayer and the laying on of episcopal hands.

One of the important aspects of ordination in the Episcopal Church is that bishops, priests, and deacons are ordained into the Church of God and nowhere is there a reference to them as ordained ministers of the Episcopal Church. The Church regards its clergy as sacramentally ordained in the One, Holy, Catholic, and Apostolic Church, not as ministers of a branch or sect of Protestantism.

As the Preface states, the background for the three orders is ancient, dating to Holy Scripture. Scripture does not discuss ordination with direct references to priests, but the New Testament refers to deacons and bishops. There are also references in the pastoral epistles to elders, in Greek presbyters (priests). The Epistle to the Hebrews portrays Christ as the great high priest, after the order of Melchizedek, an Old Testament priest, and the sacramental understanding of the priesthood links all priests to Christ.

There was a period of time between the end of the Scriptures and the apostolic tradition in which the Church was evidently ordering itself, and the three orders emerged. The orders began with the commissioning of the twelve apostles by Jesus, and their later acts are recorded in the Book of Acts when the Church in Jerusalem sent out missionaries with James, the brother of Jesus, considered by scholars to have been the first bishop.

Besides the missionary work of Ss. Peter and Paul, the Book of Acts reveals the early life of the Church and the work of the office of deacons, of which Stephen was the first:

> During this period, when disciples were growing in number, there was disagreement between those of them who spoke Greek and those who spoke the language of the Jews. The former party complained that their widows were being overlooked in the daily distribution. So the Twelve called the whole body of disciples together and said, 'It would be a grave mistake for us to neglect the work of God in order to wait at table. Therefore, friends, look out seven men of good reputation from your number, men full of the Spirit and of wisdom, and we will appoint them to deal with matters, while we devote ourselves to prayer and to the ministry of the Word.' . . . They elected Stephen, a man full of faith and of the Holy Spirit, Philip, Prochorus, Nicanor, Timon, Parmenas, and Nicolas of Antioch, a former convert to Judaism. These they presented to the apostles, who prayed and laid their hands on them (Acts 6:1–6).

Although deacons, whose title comes from the Greek *diakonia*, having to do with servanthood, waited table and distributed alms to poor widows, some also preached. Stephen was stoned to death in the midst of a sermon, becoming the first Christian martyr. In the ancient Church, deacons helped with Baptisms, pouring water over the heads of the candidates. Quite possibly female deacons served in the same role, as Baptisms were believed to have been performed separately for the two sexes.

As well as being the Church's servant-order in the

world, the diaconate has a particular service in the liturgical life. The deacon reads the Gospel, administers the chalice, and dismisses the people.

The liturgical role of the deacon has probably been best preserved by the Eastern Orthodox Churches. There, it is a permanent order, requiring a person with a good singing voice, as the deacon sings the Litany, the Gospel, and many other parts of the liturgy.

In the Episcopal Church, the diaconate is undergoing a period of reappraisal. Although it is frequently a steppingstone to priesthood, the diaconate has also become a permanent order for those who wish to serve the Church in that way. They usually serve in liturgical roles, and some have been able to combine some traditional *diakonia* with their secular vocations. They make hospital calls, visit shut-ins, take the sacrament to people who cannot get to church, and perform other pastoral duties. However, a person has to be ordained a deacon and serve in that capacity before being made a priest.

The order of the priesthood, or presbyterate, is very ancient. Originally the presbyters were a council of advisors to the bishop. They became pastors when the Church grew too large for a bishop to preside personally over the growing congregations in metropolitan areas. The priesthood thus emerged with the priest being given all of the powers of a bishop, except the right to confirm and to ordain.

The priest has the authority and power to consecrate the elements for Holy Communion, to bless and give absolution to those who are penitent and who confess their sins either during the Eucharistic ritual or in private.

The chief office in the Episcopal Church is the bishop. The name comes from the Greek, *episcopoi*, finding its way into the English, *episcopate*, from which the Church's name is derived—a Church with bishops. The concept is of the chief shepherd, or overseer, and one of the symbols of the office is the crosier, or shepherd's staff, which is carried by the bishop or his chaplain during liturgical events. The symbolism of the crosier has become less obvious in an urban society.

In addition to doing everything deacons and priests do, since he is both, the bishop confirms and ordains by rites involving the laying-on-of-hands. He is also the chief administrative officer of a diocese, presiding over the diocesan convention and important committees. If he is an assistant, coadjutor, or suffragan he will have specified jobs to perform under a diocesan bishop, but his liturgical office will be that of any other bishop.

Every priest of the Church is eligible to be a bishop; therefore there is no canonical requirement for more study or testing for consecration. A priest becomes a bishop by way of election by a diocesan convention called for the purpose. There are nominations—often through a committee as well as from the floor—speeches, and some preconvention politicking. It is considered, in spite of the politics that, finally, the election is the work of the Holy Spirit, who is quite capable of working within the political arena, either within or without the Church.

After a bishop is elected, a majority of the bishops

and of the standing committees of other dioceses must give their consent to the election. This is also true for coadjutors and suffragans. The consecration and ordination may then follow.

Some of the Scriptures used for the ordination of bishops refer specifically to the office. One of the choices for the Epistle is from I Timothy 3:1 ff. It says:

> If any one aspires to the office of bishop, he desires a noble task. Now a bishop must be above reproach, the husband of one wife, temperate, sensible, dignified, hospitable, an apt teacher, no drunkard, not violent but gentle, not quarrelsome, and no lover of money. He must manage his own household well, keeping his children submissive and respectful in every way; for if a man does not know how to manage his own household, how can he care for God's church? He must not be a recent convert, or he may be puffed up with conceit and fall into the condemnation of the devil; moreover he must be well thought of by outsiders, or he may fall into reproach and the snare of the devil.

The bishop is considered to be in the apostolic succession. That is, the line of ordination can be traced back to the apostles. Three bishops have to lay hands on the bishop-elect to make the consecration and ordination valid. Usually the Presiding Bishop, or an official appointee is one of the consecrating bishops.

During the ordination rite the Presiding Bishop says to the new bishop:

My *brother*, the people have chosen you and have affirmed their trust in you by acclaiming your election. A bishop in God's holy Church is called to be one with the apostles in proclaiming Christ's resurrection and interpreting the Gospel, and to testify to Christ's sovereignty as Lord of lords and King of kings.

You are called to guard the faith, unity, and discipline of the Church; to celebrate and to provide for the administration of the sacraments of the New Covenant; to ordain priests and deacons and to join in ordaining bishops; and to be in all things a faithful pastor and wholesome example for the entire flock of Christ.

The rite presumes that the bishop will be the chief pastor of the diocese, enabled by the renewed strength of the indwelling Holy Spirit.

The Church maintains the sacramental nature of the ministry because of its continuation from the apostles through all time. Here is the visible connection with the past; here is one unchanging element of the Church's life. No matter how ritual or ceremony changes, the sacramental priesthood has the same connections and requires the same to be valid. The Church considers that at every celebration of the Holy Communion, Christ is the chief consecrator, the host—it is Christ's banquet. The priest serves to preside over the meal, and the whole body of Christ, all those present along with "angels and archangels, the whole company of heaven" join in that celebration. A person in priest's orders must be present to consecrate the elements of bread and wine, bringing into the act the whole history of the life of the Church from the apostles' time, so that the mystery of God works to change the elements into Christ's Body and Blood.

The matter of ordination is one of the major stumbling blocks on the ecumenical scene, as the Episcopal Church will not accept Protestant ordination as valid. This does not mean that the Church questions the validity of those orders for the particular Church in which the person finds a ministry. Obviously, under that Church's polity and law the minister is validly ordained. But ordination must be performed by a bishop in the apostolic succession before a person may function in the liturgical acts of the Episcopal Church. Consequently, in ecumenical discussions, the matter of "reordination" has met with strong objection from Protestants, who hold their ordinations to be valid. They feel that submission to reordination is unnecessary and demeaning. Receiving the laying-on-of-hands in Confirmation has also been a stumbling block for people who have been confirmed in a Protestant Church, as Confirmation is also considered valid in the Episcopal Church only if performed by a bishop in the apostolic succession.

The Episcopal Church recognizes the orders of clergy in other Catholic Churches not in communion with it. Therefore, a Roman Catholic or an Eastern Orthodox priest can be received into the Episcopal Church as an ordained person, continuing the ministry, after meeting certain canonical requirements. Such clergy will be examined in certain subjects pertaining to the history and doctrine of the Episcopal Church and must accept the discipline of the Church by oath. If a bishop deems them worthy and wishes to have them function in the Episcopal Church, they are received with the right hand of fellowship, as episcopal hands have already been laid upon them in a sacramental ordination. This is not a reciprocal understanding, and Episcopal clergy who have transferred their allegiance to Rome or to one of the Orthodox Churches have had to be reordained and in the past even rebaptized. In 1896 Pope Leo XIII declared Anglican Orders invalid, but a number of Roman Catholic scholars then and now have found fault with that ruling, and it is still under discussion. The Orthodox Churches recognize only their own orders as valid.

To be ordained in the Episcopal Church, a candidate has to relate closely to the laity, as the congregation, through its elected vestry, has to agree at various points throughout the process. To a great extent, it is the congregation that is the recruiting agent for the ordained ministry. When one feels called by the Holy Spirit to seek Holy Orders the individual is "set aside," or recognized by the congregation as an applicant from within its midst. Before making such application, the candidate must speak first to the parish priest, or to a priest who can give a recommendation. It is incumbent upon congregations to seek out candidates for Holy Orders in order to assure a continuity of strong leaders in the ministry. Once accepted, the candidate usually attends a seminary for three years. Those already holding a bachelor or graduate degree receive a master of divinity (M. Div.) degree. At any time during this period a candidate may withdraw with honor and understanding.

Seminary training is not the only method of preparation, however. It is possible to read for orders with a priest, following an appointed course of study. It is also possible to be ordained as a nonstipendiary priest (one who intends to work at an outside job while serving the Church). This has been a godsend for small congregations that cannot afford a full-time ministry but desire sacramental administrations on a regular basis.

Canon Law specifies the subjects a candidate is to be examined in, including Scripture, History, Theology, and Canon Law. When sufficiently prepared, the candidate submits to an examination, one given by a local diocesan commission on ministries (priests and lay people appointed by the bishop), or the national canonical examination authorized by the General Convention in 1970.

The Church has insisted on having a highly educated and well-trained clergy, although it remains possible for non-college graduates to meet the requirements for ordination. There was a time, even in the twentieth century, when the clergy were among the most learned people of the community and were respected as much for their intellect as for their spirituality. This has changed since more people are being educated and more Church members are on an intellectual par with their priests.

After completing canonical examinations and being recommended for ordination by the local commission on ministries, the candidate has to be recommended by the standing committee before the bishop can take orders for the ordination. The candidate also has to submit to psychiatric and physical examinations in the process. From the very beginning until the day of ordination, the laity, along with the clergy, have a say in whether the person is worthy to be ordained.

Just as the road to ordination is long, the road *from* ordination is complicated. It is assumed that a sacrament is indelible and that it cannot be undone. A person may, however, formally renounce Holy Orders, thereby relinquishing the authority to minister God's word and sacraments. There are also disciplinary methods. A bishop can suspend a priest or deacon from exercising the ministry for a certain period of time.

A more stringent disciplinary action is deposition, which removes a priest or deacon from exercising the ministry indefinitely. Title IV of the Canon deals with trials and causes, and the Church has set up a system of justice which allows a priest charged and found guilty of misconduct by an ecclesiastical court to appeal. A priest pleading guilty can be deposed without trial. But unless the cause is so severe as to preclude the possibility, a deposed priest can apply for restoration of orders. There is also voluntary deposition for causes not affecting one's moral character. For instance, a priest may no longer wish to serve as an ordained person. Every diocese has a court of trial for priests and deacons, and every province has a court of review. The House of Bishops provides a court to consider charges against bishops.

A priest has an extraordinary task to meet the expectations of a congregation and to fulfill the duties required by Canon III.21. This canon also makes clear the powers of the rector of a parish, powers that are to be used with pastoral judgment. The rector has control of the worship and spiritual jurisdiction of the parish and is entitled to the use and control of the church and parish buildings "for the purposes of his office and for the full and free discharge of all functions and duties pertaining thereto. . . ."

The same Canon requires ministers in charge of parishes to instruct the children and others in the "Holy Scriptures and the Doctrines, Polity, History and Liturgy of the Church. They shall also instruct all persons in their parishes and cures concerning the missionary work of the Church at home and abroad, and give suitable opportunities for offerings to maintain that work."

Priests have the duty to instruct parents and godparents about the importance of Baptism and their obligations to the child, and to prepare young people and others for Confirmation.

Male Episcopal priests may be referred to as "Father" or "Mister" depending upon local custom. No clear custom has yet emerged with respect to female priests. Male priests may have a preference, and it is proper and traditional to use either title for them. It is not proper, grammatically, to address a priest as "Reverend," which is a word intended as a description. When a person is ordained he or she becomes "The Reverend John or Jane Doe" and is referred to in that way, or as "The Reverend Mr. or Mrs. or Miss Doe," but never as merely "Reverend" or as "Reverend Doe."

There have been married men in the priesthood since the 16th century, although some Episcopal priests prefer not to marry. Some celibate priests have entered the religious orders for men that exist within the Episcopal Church, taking the traditional vows of poverty, chastity, and obedience. The female orders were made up exclusively of laywomen until 1976 when the Episcopal Church changed its canon law to provide for the ordination of women to the priesthood. Since then some of the sisters have been ordained to the priesthood while retaining their vows.

# 7

# MISSION THEN AND NOW

MANY of the heroes of the Episcopal Church, as well as of
other Churches, emerged from the overseas mission field.
They had been sent there, or called, to proclaim the
Gospel, and in so doing they also spread American
culture and made contributions that far exceeded the
making of converts.

One of the more exciting events in the history of the
Episcopal Church's overseas mission began to unfold in
1859, when the Reverend John Liggins and the Reverend
Channing Moore Williams arrived in Japan from China,
where the Church's 20-year-old mission was beginning to
take shape. Admiral Perry had only recently visited the
shores of Japan and the doors were opening to foreigners,
although missionaries were limited to teaching English.
Williams went to Tokyo to start a divinity school, later to
become St. Paul's University.

Liggins and Williams were the first Protestant missionaries to set foot on Japanese soil since the proscription of Christianity around 1600. At that time all Christians had to leave, and an effort was made to wipe out every vestige of Christianity by means of intense persecutions, crucifixions, burnings, and tortures.

Japan first received missionaries in 1549 when Francis Xavier, a tireless Jesuit priest, moved to the islands after setting up a mission in China. By 1587 there were an estimated 150,000 Christians in Japan. But in that year an edict was issued against Christianity by Hideyoshi, the military dictator of Japan. About ten years later, missionaries were deported, and the first bloody persecutions began. Hideyoshi died in 1598, however, and Iyeyasu came to power. He removed the restrictions for a time so that by 1600 Christians in Japan probably numbered more than 200,000. The restrictions and persecutions were resumed in 1614, however, and many Christians died, some of them horribly. But just as the early Roman persecutions of the Church in the first and second centuries were unable to destroy Christianity, the proscription in Japan failed.

There were many secret Christians in Japan, and many families kept crosses within hollowed-out statues of the Buddha. When Bishop Williams went to Japan in 1868, some of these people emerged and asked for Baptism. The Christian tradition had been passed along for two centuries, not with the help of clergy or Bible, but orally and by the practice of Christian virtues, just as the tradition was communicated in the early days.

By 1882, there were about 38,000 Christians in

Japan; 200 of them were Anglicans. Growth was in evidence, and a move was made to form an independent, autonomous Anglican Church. In 1887, the constitution was drawn up for the Nippon Sei Ko Kai ("The Holy Catholic Church in Japan").

The Christian evangelizing missionaries were acting in response to the biblical injunction to "go forth and baptize." But it was also a matter of following the flag and the tradesmen. However, the evangelists who emerged after the Reformation were more serious in seeking for individual commitment than the missionaries of the Catholic Church, who "converted" barbarians of Europe with mass Baptisms after converting their prince.

It was in 1821 that the Episcopal Church gave serious consideration to missions. This was when the Domestic and Foreign Missionary Society was formed, and any member of the Church who would pay at least $3 a year could belong. There were other societies, such as the American Missionary Society, which operated similarly to the English system—raising money and sending missionaries independently of the Church.

But in 1832, the Episcopal Church made a unique change by amending the constitution of the Society so that it would include "all persons who are members of the Church." In other words, it would no longer be a society operating within the Church; the Church itself would be the Society, and all members would help the missionary activities through the operating budget. The only ground for membership was Baptism.

It seems incredible that one of the first "foreign" ventures of the Society was to send missionaries to Greece. The Reverend John J. Robertson persuaded the

Society to send a party to that ancient Christian land, and he went along with the Reverend and Mrs. John H. Hill and a printer named Solomon Bingham. The Hills operated a school in Athens until 1841, when there were between 600 and 800 students. Robertson and Bingham had a print shop in Syra and had printed 30,000 books before giving it up in 1838. The mission was closed in 1843.

This presence of Episcopal missionaries in an ancient Christian country indicates how they were setting their sights more institutionally than evangelically. So it would be for most of the Episcopal Church's ventures abroad. The missionaries have left fine schools and hospitals, some agricultural experiments such as the independent venture of Paul Rusch who founded the Kiyosoto Education Experiment Project (KEEP) in Japan, which operates a model farm and community in the mountains above Tokyo.

Even though the Church has made false starts in some places, it has had a lasting effect in others. While some Episcopal missionaries were at work in Greece in an unsuccessful attempt, a beginning was made in Liberia which was to become the oldest overseas work of the Church. The first missionary, a black layman, James M. Thompson, and his wife had come to Monrovia from Connecticut. Named to the post in 1835, Thompson died before the year was out and the Reverend Thomas S. Savage, the first white missionary sent by the Church to Africa, took his place. By 1850 the Reverend John Payne had become bishop of the whole of Liberia and there were 14 preaching stations, 240 communicants, and at least 15 schools.

Liberia's success might be weighed against another incredible effort, the mission to Turkey in 1835. The Reverend Horatio Southgate was sent to Turkey and Persia and in 1844 was elected bishop of "the Dominions and Dependencies of the Sultan of Turkey." His work among the Muslims was not successful and in 1850 he resigned and the Church withdrew from Turkey as a mission field.

When the Domestic and Foreign Missionary Society and the Episcopal Church became one and the same, another change was made to facilitate the mission. From 1835 the House of Bishops could nominate missionary bishops and the House of Deputies could elect them. This was to enable the new missions to start work with a bishop and clergy, a diocesan structure—then called a missionary district—recognizing theologically the need for a bishop as chief overseer. This has resulted in a preponderence of Americans as bishops in overseas dioceses, but since 1967, both foreign and domestic districts have been able to elect their own bishops with consent of the House of Bishops.

An American elected bishop in another province of the Anglican communion is not considered to be a member of the American House of Bishops. Although such a bishop might be given a courtesy seat and voice if present when the house meets, he would not be given a vote and would not be considered to be part of the decision-making process.

Because of the unique structure of the Anglican Communion it has been possible for the autonomous Churches to share the worldwide mission and therefore to better utilize resources. This possibility was enhanced and promoted after the Anglican Congress meeting in

St. Bartholomew's: Park Avenue, New York City
*(courtesy of Cameron R. Bloch)*

St. Bartholomew's:
Burroughs, Georgia

*William Gray*

Confirmation in the Diocese of Central Tanganyika,   East Africa

Toronto in 1964 adopted an Anglican-wide program called Mutual Responsibility and Interdependence in the Body of Christ (MRI). The Congress consisted of bishops, clergy, and lay representatives from every province of Anglicanism, and in adopting MRI they committed themselves to working out priority needs which they could share among themselves. Project lists were drawn up and the Anglican Churches could choose whatever resources, material or human, they could share. The author of MRI was the late Right Reverend Stephen F. Bayne, Jr., then Bishop of Olympia, the diocese in western Washington state, and later appointed the first executive officer of the Anglican Communion with head-quarters in London. That office coordinated the MRI program and continues to be the focal point for coopera-tion within the Anglican Communion. The American Church has, by agreement with local African provinces, sent individuals to work in certain places, in addition to its major mission in Liberia.

Even as the American Church has spawned inde-pendent Churches, notably in Japan, China, and Brazil, it has also taken at least one independent Church under its wing. That was in Haiti where, in 1861, a black American priest, the Reverend James T. Holly, went with a group of people to begin an independent mission. He estab-lished the Church of the Holy Trinity in Port au Prince, and "The Orthodox Apostolic Church of Haiti." In 1874, the House of Bishops made a covenant with the Haitian body and consecrated Holly its first bishop. He served until his death in 1911, and in 1912 the Haitian Church petitioned the House of Bishops to be taken in as a missionary district.

Although it would seem logical that the outreach of

the Church would be toward Latin America because of its geographical proximity, the outreach toward that area was relatively recent. This may have been because of the known strength of the Roman Catholic Church in the Latin American countries as well as the romantic motivation of converting "the heathen" in the Orient.

Thus in 1835 the Reverend Hanson Lockwood went to China. In 1841 he was followed by the Reverend William J. Boone, M.D., who founded the Anglican Communion in China and was elected the first bishop there in 1844. The China work was shared with other members of the Anglican Communion, notably the English, but there were American bishops present until the doors were closed in 1949 by the Communists.

Another famous name in American missionary activity is that of the Right Reverend Charles Henry Brent, who helped organize the Episcopal Church's mission in Manila in 1902. His policy was not to build altars adjacent to those of the Roman Catholic Church, and so the Philippines proved to be one place where the Episcopal Church went deep into the country seeking primary conversions. The Igorots of northern Luzon, fierce mountain tribesmen and headhunters, the Moros, Muslim people of the south around the Sulu Sea, and the Chinese in Manila, were sought out and ministered to by Episcopal missionaries.

In 1902, two years after Hawaii became a territory, the Church of England transferred its jurisdiction to the Episcopal Church. The Royal Family of Hawaii had asked Queen Victoria for Anglican clergy as early as 1860, and the first bishop, Thomas Staley, was sent there in 1862. Some clergy had accompanied the early English traders and explorers as chaplains, always leaving a vestige of Anglicanism when they departed.

Even after Hawaii and Alaska became states, they were considered to be overseas missionary districts by the Church. However, the Church streamlined its structure in 1970 and put all missionary jurisdictions, domestic and foreign, under one office, thus ending that dichotomy. In a sense, this also put all missionary efforts on the same plane in competing for money within the budget allocation for missionary work. The way the budget works at present allows for self-determinism, which is relatively new. In the past, the line-budgets were drawn up at the Church headquarters and the missionary bishops had to administer those budgets along strict lines. Missionaries were sent to the missionary bishops to work under them.

Today the districts are allocated a lump sum and the local people allocate those sums to such programs as they deem wise. Missionaries are interviewed and employed by the missionary bishop and their salaries are included in the lump sum, so that if a bishop prefers to spend that money in another way he can do so.

Alaska, too, has been an overseas post and the Church has done a lot of work among the Eskimos and Indian people of the Arctic Circle. The first missionary went there in 1867, shortly after Seward purchased the territory from Russia. The Russian Orthodox Church was there by then and sending missionaries down into Northern California. The Episcopal Church is widely scattered in Alaska, and it has been necessary for the bishop to pilot himself, or be flown, to many outposts for Confirmation and annual visitations, using planes provided by the United Thank Offering.

The Church had been interested in the Indians from colonial days, and Bishop Hobart of New York, had created a mission to the Oneidas. But the greatest work has been done in South Dakota where the Right Reverend William Hobart Hare's name is memorable. He was the 100th man to be consecrated bishop in America, and on January 9, 1873, he began his work as Bishop of Niobrara, the Indian area of South Dakota and Nebraska, including two large reservations, the Rosebud and Pine Ridge. Today some 90 Indian chapels are active and making an important contribution to the life of the Indian people. The Church, of course, moved into the other territories and has worked with Indians in Minnesota, Wyoming, Montana, Utah, Arizona, and New Mexico.

The Missionary Society began to look south of the border when it seemed the time had come to go into Roman Catholic areas. This reflected an emerging realization that the Episcopal Church could grow without engaging in proselytizing from the Roman Catholic Church. In 1857, the Constitution of Mexico was written to include a separation of Church and State, allowing for non-Roman Catholic missionaries to enter the country. In 1875 "The Mexican Branch of the Catholic Church" (Anglican) was founded, and in 1879 the Reverend Henry C. Riley was consecrated bishop. Although the Church has not grown fast in Mexico, it has grown steadily. Today the Church in Mexico has three bishops and stands a good chance of becoming an independent member of the Anglican Communion rather than a missionary district of the Episcopal Church.

The strongest work of the Episcopal Church on the South American continent was in Brazil. Brazil is now an autonomous member of the Anglican Communion, the *Igreja Episcopal Brasileira*. This was a missionary district until 1965.

Although the Church also had some success in Colombia, it has had more in Central America, especially since 1947 when the Church of England transferred Costa Rica, Nicaragua, and Northern Panama to the Episcopal Bishop of Panama. These areas, including Ecuador, now have resident bishops and Spanish ministries. Much of the work of the Church of England had been with the English settlers and West Indian Anglicans who had moved into Latin America. The American Church began to break the ice with Spanish-speaking congregations and this is now reflected in General Conventions, which often have a bilingual quality brought by Hispanic deputies.

The Episcopal Church was in the Caribbean, too, and this area is now structured into the Church as the Ninth Province. In 1904, the Reverend Albion W. Knight was elected Bishop of Cuba, and it was organized as a missionary district. The Episcopal Church had American missionaries there until the Castro revolution, and at one time had a seminary serving the area. Puerto Rico is now an independent diocese.

Members of the Episcopal Church help their Church's mission at home and abroad. Even if each individual cannot be personally involved, each person can contribute so that the Church can, in the member's name, do the work enjoined by the Bible—baptizing the whole world. The Domestic and Foreign Missionary Society regarded the world as its mission field and with meager resources did a remarkable job over the years.

The Gospel has been spread to every country of the world, and Christian nurture has often followed to form strong, indigenous Churches which are growing and which may send missionaries to the United States in the future. The Episcopal Church has played a part in all this.

But, the idea of sending missionaries abroad has waned in the face of the twentieth-century rise of nationalism and self-determinism. Instead, the Church is fulfilling its mission at home in aiding self-determination among minority peoples.

The social Gospel as a form of Christian commitment grew up with the expanding services and programs of the Episcopal Church during the early years of the twentieth century. In what has been called "an age of hopeful confidence in inevitable progress" the Church has moved forward in a wave of great popularity, sometimes actively prominent but more often not taking any lead in the movement. This comment refers to the Christian Church in general, which used books, creeds, and social agencies to put into action what it viewed as the social teachings of Jesus. The Church's asserted priority was helping to achieve self-determinism for minority peoples both at home and abroad.

Even as the Church was trying to deal with the plight of minorities in America, the Vietnam War was nibbling at its resources with growing inflation and disillusionment. Some clergy began to attack the morality of the war, creating another furor in the pews, where people had been conditioned to hearing sweet stories instead of solid sermons on the morality of the times.

Perhaps it was inevitable that the rational attempts

to deal with the technocratic revolution, civil rights, humanity, and the Vietnam War were unsuccessful; and that the way to maintain a sense of sanity and self-worth was in emotionalism and withdrawal. The word "drop-out" became familiar as youngsters found communes, yoga, marijuana, and other supports for giving up on society.

Historians may some day want to examine the 1960s as years of unrest which dramatically reshaped the Christian Church. The effect of so-called secular society cannot be thrown off, nor should it be, as technology continues to invade human concerns and man continues to use up natural resources to increase the gap between the haves and have-nots to an unconscionable distance. The process through which the Church responds to life in the 70s and 80s had its beginning in the 60s. The question becomes one of survival and at the same time one of servanthood; a question of whether the Church will try to *save* its life or *give* it for the sake of those to whom it is called to minister and proclaim the Good News.

# 8

# THE WIDER COMMITMENT OF THE CHURCH

THE Episcopal Church has been a pace-setter in the ecumenical movement, standing as it does as a bridge between Roman Catholicism and Protestantism. There is every reason to believe that the work for greater cooperation among the Churches, as well as movement toward union and reunion, will continue to be a major aspect of the Church's program.

The late Bishop Stephen F. Bayne, Jr., who earned the name "Mr. Anglican Communion" when he served as the first Anglican Executive Officer, said that the role of the Anglican Communion was to work itself out of existence. Such a statement could be interpreted to mean the end of the Episcopal Church. On the other hand, the pursuit of such a role could mean, eventually, a truly Catholic Church, representing the wide divergencies already inherent in Anglicanism but devoid of the competitive roles that keep denominations apart.

The Episcopal Church set the stage for its ecumenical involvement in 1886 when the General Convention, meeting in Chicago, issued four articles entitled the Chicago Quadrilateral. These were concepts "on which approach may be by God's blessing made towards home reunion."

It was agreed:

That the Holy Scriptures of the Old and New Testaments contain all things necessary to salvation and are the rule and ultimate standard of faith.

That the Apostles' Creed is the baptismal symbol; and the Nicene Creed is the sufficient statement of the Christian faith.

That there are to be retained two sacraments ordained by Christ—Baptism and the Supper of the Lord—ministered with unfailing use of Christ's words of institution, and of the elements ordained by him.

That the historic Episcopate should be retained, locally adapted in the methods of its administration to the varying needs of the nations and peoples called of God into the unity of the Church.

This quadrilateral was adopted by the Lambeth Conference of 1888 and renamed the Lambeth Quadrilateral. These agreements were to become the testing ground for all ecumenical endeavors and for the proposed statements of unity between any Anglican Church and any other Church holding talks of unity.

The adoption was, however, only a recommendation, as the Lambeth Conferences have no official jurisdiction over the Anglican Communion. The conferences began in 1867 and are held about every ten years at the invitation of the Archbishop of Canterbury. All the bishops of the Anglican Communion are invited, and agreements or recommendations made by such an august body will necessarily have an impact on the member Churches.

In 1920, the Anglican bishops at Lambeth issued "an Appeal to All Christian People" based on the Lambeth Quadrilateral. The nine points of the appeal embraced the quadrilateral essentials in elaborated form, beginning with an acknowledgment of "all those who believe in our Lord Jesus Christ, and have been baptized into the name of the Holy Trinity, as sharing with us membership in the universal Church of Christ which is his Body," and asking for an association "in penitence and prayer of all those who deplore the divisions of Christian people, and are inspired by the vision and hope of a visible unity of the whole Church."

With that sort of solid commitment to ecumenism, the Episcopal Church has held a number of talks with other Churches. It was not until 1960, however, following the much publicized Blake-Pike proposal, that the talks seemed to move toward consummation. The Reverend Eugene Carson Blake, then stated clerk of the United Presbyterian Church and later general secretary of the World Council of Churches, preached a sermon in Grace Cathedral, San Francisco. Blake was invited to the pulpit by the late Right Reverend James A. Pike, then Bishop of California. Bishop Pike was regarded by some as a maverick, but he was known to be a man of ecumenical sensitivity who was open to change and willing to help bring it about.

Although the Blake-Pike proposal called for a serious dialogue between the Episcopal and United Presbyterian Churches—close theologically but not liturgically and structurally—the groundwork was laid for the Consultation on Church Union (COCU), which eventually involved nine Churches: the African Methodist Episcopal; African Methodist Episcopal Zion; Disciples of Christ; Christian Methodist Episcopal; Episcopal; Presbyterian U.S.; United Church of Christ; United Methodist; and United Presbyterian in the USA. The Reverend James I. McCord, a Presbyterian at the Princeton Theological Seminary was the first chairman, and the Right Reverend Robert F. Gibson, Jr., Bishop of Virginia and chairman of the Joint Commission on Ecumenical Relations of the Episcopal Church, became its second.

Prior to the Blake-Pike proposal, a major Protestant merger had been effected, bringing together two distinct types of ecclesiastical structures. The Congregational Church (independent congregations) merged with the Evangelical and Reformed Church (connected congregations) to form the United Church of Christ, retaining the congregational structure. In the mid-1960s, the Methodist Church and the Evangelical United Brethren Church merged to form the United Methodist Church.

There were Anglican mergers abroad, notably in India, where the Church of South India emerged in the late 1950s uniting Anglicans, Methodists, Presbyterians, and Congregationalists. A great deal of controversy centered on the Church of South India, which preserved the apostolic succession with its bishops and newly ordained presbyters, but which did not require reordination of ongoing clergy from nonapostolic traditions. Since then, other unions have taken place in India, and plans for unions are well under way in South Africa.

The Consultation on Church Union was kept from becoming completely Protestant in nature by the strong Catholic influence and practice of the Episcopal Church. Agreement was reached for an episcopal structure, with bishops in the apostolic succession, and a form for the celebration of the Lord's Supper, written largely by the Reverend Dr. Massey H. Shepherd, Jr., Professor of Church History at the Church Divinity School of the Pacific, and closely resembling the Anglican liturgy. This form has been used by COCU and sometimes locally by Churches engaged in the consultation. COCU was seen by some as a plan for a super-Church not much different from its member Churches, only larger. Others saw it as a building erected from the top down which was structurally unsound. Although the drive for union has slowed, COCU has involved many people in serious ecumenical considerations that have had a lasting, historic effect on the life of the Church in the United States. As COCU continues it will provide Churches with a way to explore ecumenical cooperation, if not union.

Of course, the Episcopal Church has been engaged in ecumenical cooperation on many fronts through its membership in the National Council of Churches (NCC), the World Council of Churches (WCC), and on the local level in councils and clergy associations. The Church has been influential in all of these bodies, and an Episcopal lay person, Dr. Cynthia Wedel, served as president of the NCC from 1970 to 1972.

At the same time that the Church has been involved in conversations with many of its Protestant brethren, it

has also been involved in serious ecumenical conversations with the Roman Catholic and Eastern Orthodox
Churches, exploring theological roads to union and
reunion. These roads may eventually lead to intercommunion, but perhaps not beyond that for some time to
come. In 1971 the International Anglican-Roman Catholic Consultation issued an "Agreed Statement on Eucharistic Doctrine." If accepted by both Churches, this
would eliminate the controversy over Eucharistic faith, a
major obstacle to unity. A statement on the ministry has
also been issued in the United States. The Anglican-
Roman Catholic Consultation (ARC) has full communion
as a goal of the two Churches. There is also an
Orthodox-Anglican Consultation and a history of good
relations between various Orthodox Churches and individuals within the Episcopal Church, as well as with
other members of the Anglican Communion.

People seem to have passed over Church boundaries
to such a great extent that ecumenical action and plans
for union serve only as affirmation. Even as most
Episcopalians will not accept papal infallibility as a
condition of reunion, nor later Roman Catholic dogma
such as the bodily assumption of the Virgin Mary, many
Episcopalians now will receive Communion in Roman
Catholic Churches and Roman Catholics are visitors at
Episcopal altars. This practice and the occasional concel-
ebration of the Eucharist by Episcopal and Roman
Catholic priests are not officially condoned. The fact is
that people are finding each other, and Church loyalty is
not preventing them. The number of so-called mixed
marriages taking place in church is increasing as old
prohibitions fade.

The Episcopal Church also has good relations with Churches belonging to the wider Episcopal fellowship (See Chapter 3). The Episcopal Church has intercommunion with most of these Churches, which means that the members are free to receive Communion together.

It is also true that many Episcopalians, having come from other Churches, are comfortable in ecumenical circles because they can speak the language of both the past and the present. The Church has only to catch up with its people to discover and put forth a common, Christian mission to the world.

# BIBLIOGRAPHY

Addison, James Thayer. *The Episcopal Church in the United States.* New York: Charles Scribner's Sons, 1951. 400 pp.

Anson, Peter F. (Revised and Edited by A. W. Campbell). *The Call of the Cloister.* London: S.P.C.K., 1964. 650 pp.

Bede. *A History of the English Church and People.* Hamondsworth, Middlesex: Penguin Books, Ltd., 1955. 341 pp.

Bernardin, Joseph Buchanan. *An Introduction to the Episcopal Church.* New York: Morehouse-Barlow Co., 1957. 116 pp.

Dawley, Powel Mills. *Chapters in Church History.* Revised Edition. New York: The Seabury Press, 1963. 274 pp.

Dix, Dom Gregory. *The Shape of the Liturgy.* Westminster: Dacre Press, 1945. 764 pp.

*The Episcopal Church Annual.* New York: Morehouse-Barlow Co., 1973.

*Guide to the Religious Communities of the Anglican Communion.* London: A. R. Mowbray & Co., Ltd., 1951. 140 pp.

*Handbook on the Mission of the Episcopal Church*, No. 4, Liberia. The National Council. 123 pp.

Haugaard, William P. *Elizabeth and the English Reformation*. New York: Cambridge University Press, 1968.

Josephson, Matthew. *The Robber Barons*. New York: Harcourt, Brace & World, Inc., 1962. 474 pp.

Meagher, John. *The Gathering of the Ungifted*. New York: The Seabury Press, 1972. 176 pp.

Moorman, John R. H. *A History of the Church in England*. London: Adam and Charles Black, 1963. 460 pp.

*The Oxford Dictionary of the Christian Church*. Edited by F. L. Cross. London: Oxford University Press, 1958.

Robinson, William M., Jr., "The First Coming to America of the Book of Common Prayer: Florida, 1565." *Historical Magazine of the Protestant Episcopal Church*, Vol. XXXIV, No. 3, September 1965.

Shepherd, Massey H., Jr. *The Oxford American Prayer Book Commentary*. New York: Oxford University Press, 1950. 611 pp.

Smith, H. Robert. *The Church for You*. Greenwich: The Seabury Press, 1956. 93 pp.

Wilson, Frank E. *The Divine Commission*. New York: Morehouse Publishing Co., 1935. 296 pp.

Wilson, Frank E. *An Outline History of the Episcopal Church*. Milwaukee: Morehouse Publishing Co., 1932. 65 pp.